FROM CHARLESTON

THE BOATHOUSE

Tales and Recipes from a Southern Kitchen

TO ASHEVILLE

INTRODUCTION BY **RICHARD S.W. STONEY**
WRITTEN BY **DOUGLAS W. BOSTICK AND JASON R. DAVIDSON**

PHOTOGRAPHS BY **STEWART YOUNG** • FEATURING PAINTINGS BY **WEST FRASER**

JogglingBoardpress

CHARLESTON, SOUTH CAROLINA

THE JOGGLING BOARD

Legend has it that the idea for the joggling board came to South Carolina from Scotland in the early 1800s. The long board supported by rockers at each end allows two or more persons to rock together. This playful outdoor furniture became a common sight in the 19th century, gracing Southern porches, yards and piazzas. It was thought to be useful in easing rheumatism, aiding digestion and bolstering courtships. Some say that no daughter went unmarried in any antebellum house that was host to a joggling board.

Published by Joggling Board Press
Joggling Board Press, LLC
P.O. Box 13029
Charleston, SC 29422
www.jogglingboardpress.com

First printing 2006
Revised edition 2007
Printed in Hong Kong.

A CIP catalog record for this book has been applied for from the Library of Congress.

ISBN: 0-9753498-9-9

For my family,
the Middletons and Stoneys
and especially
Lori, Richard Jr. and Croft
and
For all the supporters of our restaurants,
without whom the journey would have been
very, very short. Amen.

TABLE OF CONTENTS

ACKNOWLEDGEMENTS

In the process of putting together this book, the project seemed at times to take on a life of its own. Through the process, I became even more aware of how special the place we call the Carolinas really is, mainly because of the sense of place that emanates from her inhabitants. It is that sense of place that we have attempted to share through the stories and recipes included in this book.

This cookbook was made possible through the efforts of many people, all contributing to make it not only a great resource for great food, but an extension of the vision we have for all the restaurants and catering that are a part of Crew Carolina.

With our management company, Crew Carolina, I would like to thank all of our employees who work so hard day after day for our organization. Thanks and recognition go to Craig Ashman, retail foods sous chef; Phil Corr, partner/executive chef – Carolina Catering; Jason Davidson, purchasing/director of retail sales; Elijah Denmark, craftsman; Nina Ita, marketing and PR coordinator; Kathy Kelly, property maintenance; Susan Landis, staff accountant; Tim Lavish, special events manager; Amy Randle, purchasing/human resources; Chip Robinson, controller; Sarah Stewart, executive assistant; and Richard Stoney Jr., retail sales and distribution.

With the Boathouse at Breach Inlet, my thanks and recognition go to Leslie Wade, general manager; Charles Arena, executive chef; Jeff Healy, assistant manager; Frank Kline, assistant manager; Andy Henderson, PM sous chef; and John Holmes, AM sous chef.

With the Boathouse on East Bay, my thanks and recognition go to Jamie Waby, general manager; Jason Ulak, executive chef; Laura Lovisone, assistant manager; Eric Winfield, AM sous chef; and Rhett Thomas, sous chef.

With the Boathouse on Lake Julian, my thanks and recognition go to Nick Linebaugh, general manager; Jeff Lanzaro, executive chef; and Nate Clark, sous chef.

At Carolina's, my thanks and recognition go to Steve Harris, general manager; Britt Wilson, assistant manager; Tin Dizdarevic, executive chef; Gavin Mills, sous chef; and Ann Stafford Ladson, pastry chef.

So many people have also contributed to making us who we are and to the look of our restaurants, including my law partners Jay Gouldon and Spence Roddey; Kirk Heidenreich, a master furniture builder; artists Jane Hurrell, Carl Flower and Desiree Laurenceau. Also Beverly Stoney Johnson, Michael Molony, Ned Payne, Croft Stoney, Laurence Stoney, Lori Stoney, Richard Stoney Jr., Ted Stoney and Tommy Westfeldt.

Helping us fulfill our promise to deliver fresh food to our customers are Adluh Mills, Buckhead Beef, Crosby's Seafood, Honolulu Fish Company, Inland Seafood, International Gourmet Foods, Limehouse Produce, Lowcountry Lobster, Mountain Food Products, Normandy Farms, Poseidon Enterprises Inc, Rawl Farms, Sunburst Trout Company, the staff at US Foods, Toby Van Buren, and Wool and Flax.

I have been fortunate to have many opportunities to travel and paint with my dear friend and artist West Fraser. In the *plein air* or open air, style, his sheer volume of work and expression are unmatched, capturing the Lowcountry, mountains and coast of South Carolina and Georgia. West's paintings are in a sense a product of his artistic evolution much the same as the Southern food, architecture and literature we speak to in the following pages. The senses contributing to the final product run deep. West is a product of the South, having grown up on a farm by a river not far from the coast. Much of his youth was spent in the woods and waterways. When he interprets with his brush those collective life experiences onto canvas, the oil images he conveys are free of gimmicks. West's art, like Southern food, makes enhancement unnecessary. I am indebted to West, his wife Helena and their gallery, Fraser Fox Fine Arts, for allowing the use of four paintings to grace this book project.

Stewart Young is the supercharged, perpetual motion machine also known to us as "Crew's photographer." I first met Stewart about five years ago, and his talent for photography is as captivating as his enthusiasm for life. Stewart has photographed a number of assignments for us, ranging from advertising shots to black and white Charleston scenes that adorn the walls of Carolina's. His photos, I am confident, will speak to you. Stewart lives in Asheville with his wife and young son. He is an avid cyclist, and adept as a mountain goat on rugged mountain terrain. To mountain bike with Stewart is an unimaginable adrenaline rush, usually followed by a post-cycling adventure such as waterfall jumping from some backwoods river.

Special thanks go to Jason Davidson, of Crew Carolina, who, in addition to his normal full load of duties, put in a great deal of time editing recipes, writing and proofing.

Jason Ulak, executive chef with the Boathouse on East Bay, was most helpful in creating, developing and tasting many of the recipes for the book.

Author Doug Bostick with Joggling Board Press is a wonderful Southern gentleman, historian, storyteller and writer who is a pleasure to work with and unquestionably has been the mainstay of this project.

This book has been elevated measurably through the editorial efforts and suggestions offered by Susan Kammeraad-Campbell with Joggling Board Press.

Courtney Gunter of Gunter Design Company deserves great credit for her design concepts and helping us to tell this story and offer our recipes in the most effective manner. Tom Smith, Ph.D., and his discerning eye reviewing our manuscripts offered us great confidence and comfort.

Thank you to Marjory Wentworth, Poet Laureate of South Carolina and publicist for Joggling Board Press, for her insights, encouragement and guidance for the book launch.

Many thanks go to Mike Coker with the South Carolina Historical Society for his enthusiastic support. As always, the many treasures of the Charleston Library Society supported our efforts to understand and define our past. Thank you to the staff of the South Carolina Room of the Charleston Public Library; the research staff with the Pack Memorial Library in Asheville, North Carolina; and the rangers with the Cradle of Forestry, Pisgah Forest, North Carolina.

We are indebted to Glenn Roberts and Dr. Merle Shepard with the Carolina Gold Rice Foundation; to Asheville food writer Rick McDaniel for his wealth of information on mountain cuisine and culture; to Danny Crooks for allowing us access to his collection of photographs of old Charleston; to my cousin David Farrow for his research and many stories about old Charleston; and, lastly, to the gracious and charming Louise Howe Bailey, Henderson County writer, historian and storyteller, for an enjoyable visit and her insights on Flat Rock.

This would not be complete without issuing an endless "hallelujah" in memory of Patrick Evan Ringwald, a devoted employee, foodie, raconteur, connoisseur of all things tasteful, especially fine wine, but most of all, our friend.

9

THE JOURNEY

This book is a confession of sorts. As with everyone, chance, circumstance and choice delivered me to this time and place. Growing up in the Carolinas has left an indelible imprint on me from which I promise never to recover. My love affair with "everything Southern" began with my first breath, taking in the Atlantic air as it carried the fertile scent of the Carolina Lowcountry. An ephemeral moment, perhaps, but growing up next to the ocean in Charleston and in the mountains of North Carolina has marked my life and defined my passions.

My wonderful parents, Lois Middleton Stoney and Theodore DuBose Stoney, raised our family on the lower Charleston peninsula on Tradd Street and "High Battery," or more properly put, East Battery. The Middleton and Stoney families have been blessed to reside in the Lowcountry across the centuries of Carolina history. They, and our kindred families – names which included Croft, DuBose, Gaillard, Hazelhurst, Marion, Means, Porcher, Robertson and Whaley – all are part of this great land.

These families, and many more like them, have deep connections to the maritime history and outdoor activities of the Lowcountry. The Middletons operated the Middleton Cotton Exchange for more than 100 years, exporting cotton throughout the world. Several Middleton ancestors were heavily involved with the blockade runners who supplied the Southern states during the "recent war of unpleasantness." In lighter times, the Middletons remained boating enthusiasts, sailing the harbor and rivers of the Lowcountry. My mother and her siblings grew up at 48 Murray Boulevard on "Low Battery," which, until the mid-20th century, had a dock with several boats of varying sizes. Like my mother and her siblings, my father and his brothers often sailed the harbor, racing their sailboat, *Eagle.*

The Stoneys were rice planters, living and farming on the upper branches of the Cooper River. My great, great grandfather Peter Gaillard Stoney planted rice at Medway Plantation from the 1830s until his death in the late 1800s. Medway was owned by the family for more than 100 years. In her book *Medway*, Virginia Christian Beach refers to Peter Stoney and his agricultural and industrial enterprises: "Peter set up the brickmaking operation adjacent to his landing on the Back River, just south of Medway house. He owned a sloop on which he transported his bricks to Charleston via Back River and the Cooper River into Charleston Harbor. In a ten-month period from 1852-1853, Peter shipped 594,000 bricks, and according to Sam Stoney, 'sent thousands down to the building of famous Fort Sumter.'"

My grandfather, Thomas Porcher Stoney, was the first in his line to "leave the land" and became a lawyer in Charleston. He was born at Medway Plantation, which, along with Gippy Plantation, further up the river, were still family working plantations at the turn of the 20th century. "Papa" purchased and sold additional plantations during his lifetime. His favorite was Kensington Plantation, also on the Cooper River, which is still owned by our family. Today, a large kitchen garden adjoining my home at Kensington supplies our restaurants with fresh regional ingredients, exotic herbs and baby vegetables.

One of our ancestors, Theodore DuBose Stoney, a businessman, was a partner in the Southern Torpedo Company of Charleston. In the early 1860s, the firm financed a series of Confederate torpedoboats known as Davids, forerunners to the *Hunley*.

From my childhood bedroom at 29 East Battery, I witnessed the daily commercial activity in the harbor and the myriad recreational watercraft as they floated across that great body of water. I listened to the early Saturday morning calls of the street merchants selling their goods – "Shrump. Shrumpman!"

Throughout the summers, my brother Ted, sister Beverly, cousin Randell (17 days my senior) and I sailed the harbor with our friends or took power boat trips with our families to the barrier islands for picnics, fishing and crabbing. My son Richard and daughter Croft were raised on Sullivan's Island and have enjoyed the Carolina coast since birth, as well as the summer mountain lakes of Kanuga, Toxaway and Summit.

Both sides of my family have had the good fortune of long connections to the mountains and the beach, with summer homes in Arden, Little Switzerland and Hendersonville, and, on the coast, at Sullivan's Island. Summer trips to my great-aunt's Hendersonville home, summer camp in Brevard, and three years of "hard time" (or boarding school, as my parents called it) in the mountains fostered an early love of the western North Carolina mountains. At all of these locations,

13

parties, large and small, offered one common denominator – Southern food, the food of my heritage.

Understanding and cooking the food of our heritage allows us to appreciate the same aromas and taste the same flavors as our ancestors. Recipes in the South are a sacred link to our forebears, passed from generation to generation like a good story. Recipes are more than a guide to preparing food; they are a record of life.

The recipes contained in this book evolved from the resources available to the people who lived and worked here. All that could be plucked, pinched, pulled, caught in a net, on a line or raked up from the pluff mud would find itself in a pot. Everything was fresh, or nearly so, because, prior to refrigeration, everything had to be prepared shortly after it was acquired. From the time of our earliest Carolina settlers in the 1670s until the advent of the "ice box" in the late 1800s, all food consisted of fresh regional ingredients or, as it is called today, "slow food."

In the South, food was and is an integral part of social gatherings. Our mild weather has influenced Southern cooking because we have been blessed with the ability to enjoy outdoor activity year around.

Some of my most powerful childhood memories stem from particular "food moments," such as my first oyster, shrimp paste sandwiches, venison, wild duck with guava jelly, boiled peanuts or shrimp 'n' grits. As in many Southern homes, shrimp 'n' grits was a staple in my house. My father, who rarely cooked anything else, loved the dish and made it for our family regularly. On most occasions, we ate it as an evening meal, usually during the colder months. It consisted of thick grits with sautéed shrimp, hot bread and a cold glass of whole milk. It was my favorite supper or "suppa" as we would say, instead of dinner or "dinna," which was served at two o'clock in the afternoon. To this day, when I order shrimp 'n' grits, I have to resist asking for a cold glass of milk.

The introductions to a new Southern delicacy or "food moments" of my youth were always during a family gathering or sometimes during more elaborate occasions, such as wedding receptions or debutante parties. As I grew older, it became obvious that the menus at these buffet-style gatherings were always dictated by primarily two factors, the type of function and the time of year. Over time, I encountered few menu surprises. By the age of 10, the ability to predict fairly accurately what I might encounter at a particular gathering never diminished my enthusiasm for the anticipated delectables. The food was consistently good, sometimes outstanding, and was always straightforward and uncomplicated. You see, my infatuation with Southern food is not just because the cuisine is the food of my heritage, but

more importantly because, in its pure form, it is completely devoid of culinary gimmicks.

The tastes, textures and smells of the two connected worlds of the Lowcountry and mountains, and the food of this amazing region have left their mark on me. I hope to convey at least some of that feeling to you through the images, recipes and stories included in this book.

Though I started my career as a lawyer, looking back it's not surprising I ended up in the restaurant business. I often refer to this decision, when asked what I do, by stating I am "running from the law." The flight began some 10 years ago or so, when I set my sights on opening my first restaurant, the Boathouse at Breach Inlet. As it evolved, the restaurant melded many of my experiences and childhood memories: my insatiable love of uncomplicated Southern food, especially fresh seafood; the culinary roots I experienced; my admiration of the artistic beauty of a fine wooden boat; and my recognition of the uncompromised and exquisite architecture of the South.

Our original slogan –"simply fresh seafood"– was and is our mission statement. As my cousin David Farrow says, "Good food is the difference between living and living well."

I invite you to take this culinary journey from the coast to the mountains. These simple, aromatic tastes are an integral part of the spirit of these places. As our authors suggest, this is history you can taste.

Richard S. W. Stoney

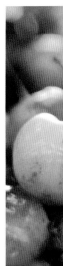

ORIGINS

No matter where you're from or where you go, food is significant to every culture and every home. Good food unites and defines us. Our need for sustenance is a given, as is our connection to food and story. Tables laden with good food sustain conversation. Smells evoke memories to be shared: What human is hardened to the scent of cornbread baking, oysters roasting, breakfast shrimp frying in bacon grease?

Charleston and the Lowcountry are steeped in history. The plateful of grits you might enjoy at the Boathouse restaurant in Charleston today is on the menu because it is connected to the past. Scroll back a century or so: In a war-ravaged city lean on resources, grits were available and cheap. Resourceful cooks developed a knack for taking this mainstay and making it exceptional through an artful marriage with other foods. Over time, those embellishments have become part of the *haute cuisine* of the region. Acts of necessity turned to acts of art. Such are the ways that food tells the story of a place.

The Boathouse: Tales and Recipes from a Southern Kitchen samples the rich broth of the past to reveal how the flavors that endure came to be here; imported, native and natural resources, even forces as seemingly alien to food as politics and religion, have determined our cuisine. Inevitably, this journey into our past heads up a well-worn path to the western North Carolina mountains. For generations, whether to escape the summertime dread of malaria, the dangers of war, or the discomfort of sweltering heat, Charlestonians have beat a path to the mountains and back. The melding that naturally comes when people and resources mix has produced a delicious array of foods and flavors.

This book is part history, part cookbook – a "cookstory" book. It is about the lure of food and the lore of food – from the Lowcountry to the mountains. Every culture has its smells and tastes. The Carolinas are a melting pot for sure – simply put, it is history you can taste.

THE GOLDEN AGE

18

Charles Towne was a great city-state born during a golden age of trading and exploration. The colony flourished in the last century of the great sailing ships (1730–1820). Charles Towne was the first stop for ships in North America following the trade winds from Europe to the Azores and West Indies. The

Carolina settlement was simply an economic enterprise. All were welcome regardless of race, creed or religion.

By the colonial era, the rice economy placed Charleston as the only major city in the South and the wealthiest in America. Planters and merchants of the city and surrounding parishes amassed fortunes that were unfathomable to all but European royalty.

Charles Towne also became an important intellectual and literary center of the colonies. Home to several newspapers and six magazines, the cultural influence in Charles Towne produced important early institutions such as the Charles Towne Library Society in 1748, the nation's third oldest subscription library; the first museum in America in 1773; and the College of Charleston in 1785.

In the mid-18th century, indigo was developed on Wappoo Creek just across the harbor from the city. Highly sought by the English to dye fabrics, indigo was a profitable complement to the rice industry, making use of the high land for a second lucrative cash crop.

By the end of the 18th century, sea island cotton was introduced, making the sea islands dotting the coast as prized as the colonial rice and indigo plantation properties up the Ashley and Cooper rivers.

Charlestonians enjoyed the finest foods and wines the world had to offer. They were well traveled and often returned home carrying a taste for the cuisine they sampled in Europe and the Mediterranean. Early Charleston receipt books reflect German, Spanish, French and Italian influences.

A CULTURAL GUMBO

The number and combination of cultures that found their way to Charleston all contributed to a distinctive regional cuisine. Lowcountry cuisine was born of water, from the ocean to the swamps. The fresh fish of the waterways and an abundance of shellfish inspired dishes such as turtle soup, shrimp pilau and she-crab soup.

Food is the only element in our culture that reaches our consciousness through all five senses: feel the texture, see the colors and shapes, hear it cook, smell the aroma, taste it.

- John Egerton

Native Americans introduced corn, beans, strawberries, muscadines, scuppernongs, sweet potatoes, sweet peppers, pumpkins and squash to the early colonists. Early English settlers also found the peaches and figs left in the Carolinas by early Spanish explorers. They brought cattle, goats, sheep and chickens. Scots settled in Charleston in large numbers in the mid-18th century, introducing puddings, stack cakes, soups, stews and pies to the cuisine. Many Europeans who settled in Charleston were families who first migrated to the islands of Barbados, Antigua, St. Christopher's and Bermuda. During the same period, almost half of all whites in the port city were French Huguenots. Charleston also contained the largest Jewish population in the colonies. All contributed their foods and culinary knowledge to the mix that was becoming Lowcountry cuisine.

While many cultures contributed to Charleston's culinary evolution, none was more influential than the West African.

Rice cultivation required substantial labor and Carolina planters turned to the slave trade to provide it. While the specter of slavery lingers, the contributions of African culture are profound. Slaves brought peas, okra, benne seeds and the knowledge and experience to grow rice. White Charlestonians may have recorded the recipes in their journals, but black Charlestonians developed, embellished and prepared them.

Rich or poor, black or white, most Charlestonians enjoyed rice and/or grits at every meal. Likewise, everyone enjoyed crab and shrimp from the waterways and happily sat down to a meal of Hoppin' John, okra gumbo or shrimp pie. No one group holds the exclusive claim to Lowcountry cuisine.

TO THE SALT OR TO THE PINES

By the 1790s, malaria and the summer fevers in Charleston were taking a toll on planters and their families. West African slaves appeared to be immune. Doctors theorized that the fevers were borne by the atmosphere. Famed architect Robert Mills wrote in 1826 that the fevers were due to the "nocturnal fogs of the swamps and lowlands." Dr. S.H. Dickson, addressing the South Carolina Agricultural Society in 1843, wrote, "The beautiful and fertile Lowcountry of our State is the seat of annual and endemic visitations of disease, which we are accustomed to attribute to Malaria. Whatever may be the difference of opinion elsewhere as to the source of origin of the aerial poison, the Medical Profession here is unanimous in regarding it as the result of vegetable decomposition in moist places at a high temperature ... ." Even as Charlestonians swatted away the hordes of mosquitoes in the lowlands, no one understood these biting pests were the root of the summer fevers.

19

An old Charleston proverb swears that "Carolina is in the spring a paradise, in the summer a hell, and in the autumn a hospital." While no one understood the cause of the "summer sickliness," white families began a tradition of leaving the plantations from mid-May to mid-October, returning only after the first frost. Initially, families went to the salt (ocean-front) or to the pines in new villages like Pineville, McPhersonville, Hardeeville and Summerville, where they built summer homes.

On the coast, new communities such as Moultrieville (Sullivan's Island), Johnsonville and Riversville (James Island), Legareville (John's Island), Rockville (Wadmalaw Island) and Edings Bay (Edisto Island) were established. By 1826, Moultrieville had more than 200 homes, most only occupied during the summer. Sullivan's Island was home to four luxurious hotels – Jackson's, The Planter's, The Point House and The Moultrie House.

Opening in 1859, The Moultrie House was built on the beachfront with a view of Charleston and an observatory looking out to the sea. The hotel boasted an enormous front piazza, a 2,500-square-foot ballroom, billiard tables, bowling

> *The lands are laden with plenty of corn, pompians [squash], water-mellons, mush-mellons . . . The country abounds with grapes, large figs and peaches; the woods with deer, covies, turkeys, quails, curles, plovers, herons . . . oysters in abundance with a great store of mussels; a sort of fair crabs and a round shell-fish called horse-feet.*

- William Hilton in 1664 on a voyage to the Carolina coast

salons, carriage rides on the beach and boats for an afternoon of fishing. The *Charleston Courier* reported the kitchen stocked "every delicacy of the markets of New York, Havana, Key West and Charleston could furnish."

As early as 1765, some South Carolina planters summered in Newport, Rhode Island. John Ball Jr. noted in 1827, "Newport is certainly the most pleasant summer climate, I believe, in the United States. If you are fond of shooting you can exercise without the risk of overheat and find plenty of Plover on the Island or if you prefer fishing and sailing, Newport Harbor is a delightful place for such amusements." By the 1830s, so many Lowcountry planters summered in Newport that *New England Magazine* referred to Newport as "South Carolina, No. II."

LITTLE CHARLESTON

At the turn of the 19th century, businessmen were keenly interested in building roads to connect Charleston to western North Carolina and on to Tennessee and Ohio, creating business for the Charleston port. Plans were made as early as 1819 to build the Saluda Gap Road along an old trading path across the mountains to Buncombe County, North Carolina. In 1827, the road finally opened.

Many Lowcountry residents quickly found the summer climate in the western North Carolina mountains appealing. Charles Baring, a Combahee River planter, established a 4,000-acre mountain estate at Flat Rock in 1830. He was followed by Judge Mitchell King, a lawyer and probate judge, who built his home "Argyle" in 1837. Mountain estates were soon built in Flat Rock by Charlestonians Thomas and Richard Lowndes, Daniel Huger, Christopher G. Memminger and Rev. John Grimke Drayton.

Grove Park Inn Fireplace.

©J.W. Pelton
1913
Asheville, N.C.

Of course, they brought with them their traditions. In time, Flat Rock came to be known as "Little Charleston." Charles Baring and his wife built a small chapel on their property that, after remodeling in 1854, was named St. John–in-the-Wilderness. Charleston Rev. Charles Cotesworth Pinckney and Rev. John Grimke Drayton, owner of Magnolia Plantation on the Ashley River outside of Charleston, served as rectors for the summer services in the early years of the church. St. John continued to be open only in the summer until 1958.

In 1850, Henry Farmer, a Lowcountry rice planter, built the Flat Rock Hotel for summer guests. Every day, he operated a four-horse carriage to and from Greenville, South Carolina, transporting guests arriving from Charleston by train. Not everyone appreciated the arrival of the summer residents in May of each year. In 1836, Benjamin Perry complained in his diary, "They all seem disposed to gratify their animal propensities without cultivating their interests at all, if they have any to cultivate – drinking, eating, gambling and whoreing [sic] is the summit of their ambition."

Southern food is not just food cooked south of the Mason-Dixon line. It is a product of time and people as well as place.

- Bill Neal

Two Charlestonians are at the center of a captivating legend about Flat Rock. Christopher G. Memminger of Charleston and Flat Rock was secretary of the treasury of the Confederacy from 1861 to 1864. He was succeeded by George Trenholm, who served to the end of the war. As Richmond was about to fall into Union hands, Jefferson Davis and key members of the Confederate government fled south. Memminger suggested

that Flat Rock serve as the interim capital of the Confederacy, a proposal that was not adopted. On the evacuation of Richmond, the remaining gold in the Confederate treasury and the "Great Seal of the Confederacy" were removed. Stories have persisted through the years that Memminger and Trenholm, whose brother Edward had an estate in Flat Rock as well, hid those items in "Little Charleston." The "Great Seal of the Confederacy" finally did turn up and is now in the Museum of the Confederacy in Richmond. The lost Confederate gold is, alas, still lost.

Not until 1878 did rail service make it across the Saluda Gap and up to Flat Rock, Hendersonville and Asheville, making the mountains much more accessible. From the street names of Flat Rock to the pews and headstones of St. John-in-the-Wilderness, the names of Charleston families pervade. Charlestonians are still "summering" in the mountains.

As Charleston has traditions, so do her sister communities in western North Carolina. For centuries, Charlestonians have steeped themselves in mountain life. The spectacular vistas of the Appalachians contrast with the flat horizons of the ocean and the Lowcountry. The uplands wear the seasons more sharply. The greens of summer give way to the burnished reds and ochre yellows of fall – colors that stir the heart. Charlestonians and other "summer people" have influenced the flavor of communities like Flat Rock and Saluda. Just as important, but often overlooked, are the influences the mountain people and their communities have had on the "summer people."

PRESERVING CHARLESTON CUISINE

In the 18th and 19th centuries, Charleston families maintained books of "receipts," an older term meaning recipes. These heirlooms became the repository of how to's, tips, remedies and recipes. Delectable favorites such as shrimp paste, pickled shrimp, okra gumbo, shrimp pilau, country captain, pickled watermelon rind, Charlotte Russe, hog's head stew and turtle soup were all written and passed from generation to generation, even though in most families these foods were prepared by slaves and, later, black servants.

Beyond recording recipes, the journals preserved home remedies for the woman of the house to use in running the household. Receipts to make writing ink, homemade night lights, cement to repair the hearth, dyes for clothes, potions to remove stains, salt and kerosene solutions to kill bed bugs, powders to discourage ants, deer skin to wash windows, and a host of formulas to make soap were all common in these journals.

If a daughter or granddaughter needed a remedy to treat a member of the family, the cure could be found in the family receipt book. Receipts for treating the "flux," gout, hiccough, "scald head," "dropsy," "jaw fallen in children," "pain in the face," and to end a "purging" could all be found.

Some of these early family receipt books have survived, offering wonderful insights into the history of Charleston cuisine. The earliest known Charleston book was Eliza Lucas Pinckney's recipe book, circa 1756. Born in the West Indies, Eliza Lucas was moved by her father, a British army officer, to Charleston in 1738. Her father was later called back to Antigua and, in his absence, Eliza ran the family plantation on the Wappoo Creek. As a teenager, she experimented with indigo seeds sent to her by her father and perfected a dye that became a lucrative export for South Carolina planters.

In 1744, she married Charles Pinckney, chief justice for the colony. She soon became the manager of his plantations in the Lowcountry. Her sons, Charles Cotesworth Pinckney and Thomas Pinckney, were both generals in the Revolutionary War. Charles was a signer of the United States Constitution and Thomas later became United States Minister to Spain and Great Britain.

Her book carefully recorded many of the early classic Lowcountry recipes. She also copied all her correspondence in a letterbook that was published in 1850, providing remarkable insights into life in early Charles Towne. Eliza died in 1793 and was buried in Philadelphia, taken there for treatment for an illness. At his own request, President George Washington served as a pallbearer.

Recipe for Writing Ink: Boil ripe elderberries in water until you obtain liquid of a rich color. Then in a small quantity of copper, strain and set aside for a day or two before using.

- DuBose family receipt, early 19th century

The first published South Carolina cookbook was Sara Rutledge's *Carolina Housewife* in 1847, published for charity. She was the daughter of Edward Rutledge, one of South Carolina's signers of the Declaration of Independence. Her recipes included dishes with Italian, French and German influences as well as many classic Lowcountry dishes such as Hoppin' John and benne soup. She offered delightful recipes for eggnog, Bavarian cream and Charlotte Russe that have guided Lowcountry cooks for generations. Her cookbook included more than 300 recipes using rice or corn, and 30

24

recipes for rice breads alone, a clear demonstration of the importance of these crops. *Carolina Housewife* could be found in kitchens across the southeast.

Another book of receipts, called the *Carolina Rice Cook Book,* documented a host of rice recipes just before the rice industry met its demise in Charleston. Mrs. Samuel G. Stoney compiled the *Carolina Rice Cook Book* for the South Carolina Interstate and West Indian Exposition, Charleston's "world's fair," which ran from December 1, 1901, to May 31, 1902. The 100-page cookbook was a popular souvenir for the nearly 700,000 who attended.

Just 10 years later, on August 28, a major hurricane hit Charleston, destroying the entire rice crop just before harvest. The rice fields were covered in salt water – an assault from which the rice industry never recovered. Ironically, the success and wealth derived from the rice was due to the work and expertise of slaves brought to America in bondage. Charleston blacks referred to this devastating storm as the "Duncan Storm." A young black man had been hanged just

weeks before for a murder the city's black population believed he did not commit. They believed the cyclone that destroyed the rice was God's retribution on Charleston for hanging an innocent man.

A cookbook entitled, *Old Receipts from Old St. John's,* was compiled in the early 20th century in Pinopolis, South Carolina. The surviving work, now a tatter of pages crudely bound, was the effort of a handful of folks from an old Southern community to keep alive the good food they knew so well. In the forward, editor Anne Sinkler Fishburne wrote, "An Epicure sighingly [sic] remarked that one of the serious calamities brought about by the surrender at Appomattox was the disappearance of Southern Cookery. Surely this is an exaggeration, but lest it should come true, shall we not endeavor to preserve the recipes which would otherwise soon be but a memory?"

Perhaps the one cookbook that has done the most to preserve Lowcountry cuisine was first published in 1950. The Junior League of Charleston published *Charleston Receipts,* a compilation of recipes from most of Charleston's historic families. The fascinating book included 350 receipts, Gullah

United to one another as we were by the ties of blood and tradition, the outstanding feature of our neighborhood was the true spirit of hospitality.

- Old Receipts From Old St. John's, circa 1919

verses and illustrations of the historic city. The project, chaired by Mary Vereen Huguenin and Anne Montague Stoney, was a raging success, selling the entire print run of 2,000 books in just two days. The book was a fundraising project benefiting the Charleston Speech and Hearing Center. *Charleston Receipts* is in its 32nd printing and has sold, to date, nearly one million copies.

CHANGING TIMES

Immediately after the Civil War, times were very hard in Charleston. Despite the bounty that nature had provided for centuries, war had ruined the plantation fields. Whites lacked labor, cash, and, in some cases, expertise to rejuvenate their plantations. Blacks were exhilarated with the prospects of freedom. But farming was all the many freed people knew, and they lacked land and cash for seed. Slowly, the agrarian economy struggled to its feet. Planters who once cultivated hundreds or thousands of acres, however, could only organize to return one-tenth of the land to production. Rice, corn and peas were, sometimes, all that was available to eat.

It was during this time of great poverty and limited resources that Southern food consisted of basic foods, inexpensively prepared. The tired myth that Southern food is mostly fried, high in carbohydrates and empty calories is derived from this relatively short post-war era. It's a myth that does a disservice to centuries of fine cuisine.

Eventually Charleston revived itself – fishermen brought their catches to market, fields yielded enough crops for sale and wild game returned to the countryside. Rice and cotton – the great cash crops – however, would never reach their pre-war levels. While farmers experimented with a great variety of crops, nothing generated the return that rice and cotton

had. In 1911, rice cultivation ended and, by 1920, it was clear that cotton would not survive its struggle with the boll weevil. Noted Lowcountry author Herbert Ravenel Sass wrote, "Sea Island cotton had vanished as though some evil magician had waived his wand and conjured it out of existence."

From the end of the Civil War until after World War II, Charlestonians possessed little in the way of material wealth. They did, however, enjoy their traditions. Seasonal crops were plentiful, and the enduring Lowcountry cuisine was served among the ruins. The devastation of war and the collapse of the economy could not deter what has become an ineluctable fact: Through time, Charleston and New Orleans, the two major ports in the Southern United States, have defined Southern cuisine – a blend of three cultures: European, African and Native-American. It's the unwavering devotion to tradition and locally raised ingredients that give Lowcountry food its inimitable character.

Charleston's lingering destitution had a corresponding benefit. She remained relatively uninfluenced by fads. Betty

Hamilton, the late daughter of Charleston artist Elizabeth O'Neill Verner, once remarked that Charleston was like a crowded raft – each person kicking in his own direction in such a way that the raft stood still.

Through the mid-1970s, it was not uncommon to have shrimp and grits for breakfast. Or is it shrimp and hominy? Many people from "off" inquire as to the difference. The truth is, today, most Charlestonians don't know. No matter the name, the popularity for the dish stemmed from its low-cost accessibility. The same was true of shrimp. The delectable crustaceans were plentiful and cheaper than meat and fish.

The streets of Charleston, through the mid-20th century, witnessed a daily parade of African American hucksters peddling their products pushed on a cart or balanced on their heads. Maids in starched uniforms awaited their arrival to stock the house with foods and flowers. Each of these entrepreneurs offered a song or rhyme while enroute to advertise their offerings. These "cries" were, at times, folk songs sung in Gullah, the rich blend of dialects common to the Lowcountry.

Not long after the sun broke the horizon across the harbor, the first of the salesmen would arrive with cries of "Swimpy, Swimpy," echoing through the streets. The shrimp men sold their *fruits de mer* for 10 cents a plate, a plate being roughly equal to a pint.

Closely following the shrimpmen came the hucksters, selling fish and oysters. The cart man might sing, "Porgy walk, Porgy talk, Porgy eat with a knife and fork." He'd be offering porgy, a prized saltwater chub.

One fish huckster named Joe Cole rolled his cart through the streets singing:

> *Old Joe Cole – Good old Soul*
> *Porgy in the Summertime*
> *An e Whiting in de Spring*
> *8 Upon a string.*
> *Don't be late, I'm watin' at de gate.*
> *Don't be mad – Here your shad*
> *Old Joe Cole – Good Old Soul.*

In the daily ritual, after the fish hucksters came the vegetable vendors. Rather than haul carts, these talented saleswomen balanced large baskets on their heads filled with the fresh produce brought in from the sea islands by boat overnight. These baskets, weighing as much as 50 pounds, did not deter the hucksters from making their appointed rounds, singing, "Vegetubble, get yo vegetubble."

In the springtime, uniformed maids would scurry to the gate after hearing:

> *Straw – BER – ry,*
> *e fresh an e fine,*
> *an e jus off de vine,*
> *Straw – BER – ry.*

The last of the daily cavalcade would be the flower ladies. These hucksters ensured that the old, sometimes crumbling, homes of the peninsula city were made more inviting with fresh flowers. One native Charlestonian recalled that the flower ladies would sometimes chastise the maid who passed them by without purchasing by singing, "What's wrong with the lady at 84? How come she don't buy my flower no mo?"

As health laws became more stringent and refrigeration improved, the arrival of grocery stores put the hucksters out

29

of business. Southern food changed with the advent of the gas stove, refrigeration and improved transportation. Not all innovations are improvements. All that is left of the hucksters' processional are the echoes of their songs.

The lone vestige of the street hucksters are the basket ladies in the market and at the "Four Corners of Law" at Broad and Meeting streets in Charleston. The same baskets that once bore the morning flowers or strained to hold the "vegetubbles" balanced on the head, became the next industry for the African Americans who made them. As florists and full-service grocery stores could offer a greater variety of flowers than the street hucksters, the flower business died. Now you'll find sweetgrass baskets and popcorn wreaths offered at the "Four Corners."

LOWCOUNTRY IN TRANSITION

For centuries, Lowcountry blacks created, concocted and prepared the local cuisine. In Charleston during the segregation of the 20th century, whites and blacks ate the same food, just not together. Following segregation, "whites are not the only customers and blacks are not the only cooks," wrote John Egerton, a popular food writer. Everyone continued to cook and eat what they knew – Lowcountry cuisine.

As a port city, Charleston was historically awash in taverns. In the early 20th century, there were more than 300 "blind tigers," bars operating in defiance of state and federal liquor laws. The indigenous cuisine, though, was largely prepared in the homes, hotels and private clubs of the city. Even through the late 1960s, fine dining in Charleston was limited to three restaurants – Perdita's (now Carolina's), Henry's and the Colony House, all now long gone. "Seafood shacks," small,

somewhat obscure, coastal establishments, spanned the culinary hallow during those years. By the late 20th century, restaurants were plentiful in Charleston, and Lowcountry cuisine, available to the public outside the home, experienced a revival.

Southerners love a good story, and indigenous food is a story you can eat. Lowcountry and mountain residents alike have opinions about their food – all of it. They focus not only on what they eat and how it's cooked, but where it comes from. They pride themselves on knowing which farmer has the best silver queen corn or the sweetest tomato. Heated conversations have erupted at oyster roasts over whether the best tasting oysters come from Bulls Bay or the Folly River. Decisions about the preferred pickled shrimp recipe or who makes the best artichoke relish can rise to the same fiery level of debate as contrary opinions about politics or religion.

As our society becomes more and more mobile, the distinctive character of any region can be diluted. But Charleston, like New Orleans, is one area in which many of the idiosyncratic features of the culture have held. Charleston's past is preserved in her architecture and lingers in the Gullah patois and the Charleston mannerisms that endure. And the food – well, that's what this book is all about. How the traditions and the recipes grew from a polyglot of forces – a confluence of cultures, a region rich in natural and human resources, a history formed by the forces of extraordinary wealth and extreme privation.

A good meal with family helps define our lives. It's not only the rich smells and tastes, but the sounds of family and friends telling tales, imprinting our palates and our memories – indeed, forming our lives.

SPRING

Spring arrives in Charleston with all the enticements desired by any Chamber of Commerce. By mid-march, as the sun-warmed breezes waft through narrow streets and alleys, tea olive perfumes the air. The azaleas are a welter of color accented by the vivid whites and pinks of dogwood blossoms. Aged houses offer a distinguished backdrop to the formal gardens bursting with spring blooms. It is the reason that thousands of visitors flock to the city of Charleston each year. The Festival of Houses and Gardens, a tour of Charleston homes and gardens held annually since 1947, is a favorite destination event.

With spring comes the new crop of fresh vegetables. Asparagus and strawberries offer the first tastes of the season. One of the world's oldest cultivated vegetables, asparagus was grown in the Mediterranean and Asia Minor as far back as 2,000 years ago. The spears made their way to America by the late 17th century. Once exposed to the vegetable, Native Americans dried asparagus for medicinal use in the treatment of bladder, kidney and heart problems.

Three Sisters

Early settlers in the western North Carolina mountains learned many planting techniques and survival lessons from the Cherokee. Among the most beneficial was companion planting, the best example of which was known as the Three Sisters (corn, beans and squash).

As winter faded and spring arrived, the Cherokee buried fish and planted corn in the same spot. The fish provided important nitrogen, fertilizing the corn. When the corn sprouted, pole beans were planted alongside the corn stalk, serving as a trellis. Finally, squash was planted, providing shade and trapping moisture for all three plants.

The Three Sisters were planted together, eaten together and celebrated together.

The sweet, juicy strawberry was already in the young colony when colonists arrived, cultivated by Native Americans. They ate ripe berries, but also cooked with them. Crushed strawberries were mixed with cornmeal and baked into a bread – perhaps an early strawberry shortcake. Today, strawberry farms opening for "u-pick-it" days announce spring for everyone from school kids on field trips to grandmothers eager to make their annual batches of strawberry jam.

Spring also rewards patient fishermen and culinary enthusiasts. Mackerel and seabass arrive off the coast in March. On South Carolina's artificial reefs, anglers enjoy catches of red and black drum and porgy. Inshore, flounder, stripers and bluefish abound. In the mountains, trout begin to move as the waters of the streams and creeks warm.

In the western North Carolina mountains, the annual arrival of whippoorwills signals the advent of spring and the planting season. Early mountain settlers were Scot-Irish and German. Of course, the Blue Ridge Mountains had long been the home of the Cherokee, who called the area "Shaconge" – meaning "mountains of the blue smoke." Much of the early mountain cuisine, as in the Lowcountry, was adapted from the Native Americans.

Typical mountain spring crops were corn, beans, squash and melon. Germans brought a taste for dumplings, stack cakes, krauts and apple-butter. The Scot-Irish quickly learned to adapt from oat porridge to corn pudding. Learning from the Cherokee, sassafras tea became a popular spring tonic. A popular mountain saying was, "Drink sassafras during the month of March, and you won't need a doctor all year."

The mountains also shared a common proclivity with the Lowcountry – a large breakfast to start the day. Waffles, biscuits, hotcakes, bacon, sausage and eggs with pork brains were all common. The biggest difference was grits, with or without shrimp. Other than in "Little Charleston," the dedication to grits did not make its way to the mountains until the mid-20th century.

The South was home to three anadromous species of fish – herring, sturgeon and shad. These fish live in the open sea, but swim into the fresh rivers to spawn. Today, herring are rarely found further south than North Carolina.

THE BOATHOUSE *Tales and Recipes from a Southern Kitchen*

Through the mid-20th century, the fresh water rivers of the South Carolina coast were filled with 12- to 15-foot sturgeon moving in to spawn. These prehistoric-looking creatures of the sea were highly sought for their roe, used to make caviar. A mature sturgeon cow can yield as much as 3 million eggs.

In 1985, the State of South Carolina closed the coast to sturgeon fishing after the population was severely depleted by pollution, dam construction and over-fishing on the rivers needed for spawning. Sturgeon are now on the comeback. Recent sightings by fishermen report sturgeon greater than seven-feet long in the Edisto River. There are no immediate plans, however, to re-open the South Carolina coast to harvest them again. Caviar lovers await.

While sturgeon roe can no longer be harvested on the coast, several enterprising fishermen are experimenting with mullet caviar. In the mountains, trout caviar is growing in popularity.

The third anadromous fish, called shad, is still widely available. Like the sturgeon, shad is a bony fish and therefore not popular for its meat. But shad roe, the eggs of the fish, has been a March favorite of Lowcountry gourmets for three centuries. The roe come in a sack and, when prepared correctly, offer a meal as good as you'll ever eat. Shad appear as soon as the coastal waters warm in the spring. They are available for just under two months before moving north.

For two generations, folks from across the Lowcountry would make a 30-mile pilgrimage down Savannah Highway (U.S. 17 S.) to Jacksonboro's Edisto Motel Restaurant, famous for its shad roe. Even on days when the service was slow, the food was worth the wait. Wrapped in bacon, fresh roe from the nearby Edisto River was a delight.

As Interstate 95 became available to north-south traffic, many out-dated tourist courts along Highway 17 became superfluous. Even after the Edisto Motel closed around 1980, the restaurant, attractive because of its fresh, local food, managed to hold on for nearly two decades. The Boathouse restaurants are proud to carry on this spring tradition with their own version of shad roe (pg. 48).

35

The exchange of delicacies and first fruits of the season was one of the gracious and kindly customs and much skill went into the concocting of dishes sufficiently delectable to tempt the most jaded palate.

– From *Old Receipts from Old St. Johns,* circa 1919

Springtime also brings with it the horse racing season. Each April, the Carolina Cup is considered a rite of spring: 50,000 to 70,000 people from all over the Southeast descend on the small town of Camden, South Carolina. The Cup, established in 1930, is as big in the Palmetto state as the Derby is in Kentucky, as much a nod to fashion and food as it is a sporting event.

Usually surpassing 50,000 people, crowds arrive in everything from formals to shorts and sandals. Large tents appointed with white tablecloths and candelabras are common. Walking through the infield is to witness thousands of grills and hundreds of bartenders pressed to their functional limits.

Tailgaters enjoy crab imperial, crab cakes, shrimp paste sandwiches, blue cheese coleslaw and pimento cheese (the paté of the South) served in more ways than you can imagine. The announcer's descriptions of the thoroughbreds on the track barely make a ripple above the thousands of conversations hovering over an impressive array of food and drink.

Each April, Tryon, North Carolina, boasts its own race at the Block House Steeplechase, sponsored by the Tryon Riding and Hunt Club. Founded by Carl P. Brown in 1925, the Tryon Riding and Hunt Club, Inc., promoted horseback rides and picnics, helping maintain hundreds of miles of riding trails and equestrian events. The club was incorporated in 1960 as a nonprofit organization. The Block House Steeple Chase is as famous in western North Carolina as the Carolina Cup is for its Southern neighbors. The same finery and food pervades – a medley of smells from tangy barbeque to mint juleps and horses.

The Boathouse restaurants honor the tradition of the spring races with our own tempting recipes. Meeting Street Crab Imperial (pg. 48), Stone Crab Claws (pg. 53) and Boathouse Crab Cakes (pg. 56) will make your party the envy of tailgaters nearby.

Charleston is known as a city of "firsts." The first fire insurance in North America was offered in 1736; the first golf club in North America, formed in 1786; the first scientific observations about weather, recorded by Dr. John Lining, starting in 1737;

Soft Shell Crab
A coastal delicacy

Nature offers a treat for crab lovers in early May, when the blue crab molts its hard shell. Molting crabs seek shallow water to hide in the debris and grass at the shoreline. Once a crab discards its hard shell, it is weak and cannot deftly move or swim. A generations old process known as scapping has been popular in retrieving these crabs. In a small boat, two men move along the shoreline – one uses a long pole to move the boat while the other stands on the bow with a long-handled dip net. As the crabber spots the crab in the early morning light, he scoops it up and into the boat.

The soft shell crab season typically lasts six to eight weeks. Today, frozen soft shell crabs are available year around. Still, nothing beats the taste of a fresh soft shell crab plucked from the ocean. If you cook your own, remember, the simpler the better – don't mask the sweet taste of the crab. Soft shell crabs are best sautéed or lightly dusted in breading and fried.

Carolina Caviar

Historically, there were three anadromous species of fish that visited the Carolina coast each spring to spawn – herring, shad and sturgeon.

Sturgeon hold the greatest mystique of the three, fascinating fishermen and diners alike for centuries. Native Americans fished for these prehistoric creatures, an ancient fish believed to date back 70 million years. In the 18th and 19th centuries, the rivers along the South Carolina coast were filled with 10- to 12-foot Atlantic sturgeon, weighing up to 1,000 pounds. One elder Carolinian said of the early 20th century, "ducks were so thick in the air they blotted out the sun and sturgeon were so plentiful in the water you could walk on their backs." Okay, perhaps a slight exaggeration, but even as recently as 1976, 55 percent of all sturgeon harvested on the east coast came from South Carolina.

So thick was the skin of the sturgeon, it was used to produce "leather" for clothing and bookbinding in the colonial era. It also yielded highly prized meat and plentiful roe, which produced delicious, high-quality caviar. Winyah Bay, north of Charleston, produced more caviar than any other port on the east coast.

the first manufactured ice, made by John Gorrie in 1851; the first interior bathtub with running water; the first tea planted in the United States in 1802; the first prescription drug store in 1780; the first cotton mill on James Island in 1789; and the list goes on.

There is one Charleston "first" that most people don't know about. The "cocktail party" had its origin during the Charleston Renaissance of the 1920s. Until the modern world descended upon Charleston after World War II, businesses and banks closed at 2 o'clock, and Charlestonians went home for "dinner," the main meal of their day. In the evenings, families had a light supper, which could be anything from soup and sandwich to leftovers.

Because the servants went home in the afternoon, most wealthy Charlestonians avoided entertaining in the evening. Many newcomers and visitors alike took this as an affront – that Charlestonians chose not to mingle with them. A Charlestonian residing on Legare Street invited a small gathering of native Charlestonians and newcomers for punch and cocktails. This alone was nothing new. Charleston had a long tradition of inviting friends in for a drink. Her simple innovation was to set up finger food for her guests – shrimp paste sandwiches, crab claws, benne seed wafers, cheese wafers and pickled shrimp. There were no plates set out, thus limiting what needed to be cleaned. The "cocktail party" was a hit and quickly spread throughout the city. Today, cocktail parties offering finger food are commonplace across the country.

Charleston has never been quick to change anything. An editorial in the Charleston *News and Courier* in 1910 chastised Atlanta businessmen for not closing at 2 o'clock. The editorial writer surmised these "extended" business hours were motivated by greed. He offered, "If you were to toss a nickel in the busiest Atlanta intersection, the men would injure each other in pursuit." By the later part of the 20th century, however, the 2 o'clock dinner became a thing of the past as businesses remain open all afternoon. The big meal of the day shifted to evening. The practice of the cocktail party, however, endures, perhaps observed at its best during Charleston's annual Spoleto Festival.

Twentieth century Charleston has a long history with city festivals, in part to promote the city. Perhaps this history originated with the 1901-02 South Carolina Interstate

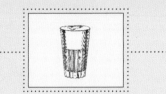

Iced Tea

Folks from the mountains and the Lowcountry share a passion with the rest of the South for iced tea, especially sweet iced tea. Charleston was the first place in the United States to grow tea. In 1795, French explorer and botanist Andre Michaux brought many varieties of camellias, gardenias and azaleas to Middleton Barony on the Ashley River.

Initially, green teas mixed with liquor were used to make party punch, such as Charleston's famed St. Cecilia Punch. Recipes for sweet tea began to appear by 1879, and, in 1884, a recipe was printed using black tea to make iced tea, the way it is most often enjoyed today. By 1900, recipes for iced tea were common. In the South, unlike other regions, iced sweet tea is consumed for lunch and dinner, year around.

Today, Charleston has the only tea plantation in America, located on Wadmalaw Island. The plantation was started as an experimental project by Lipton Tea in the 1960s. Later, it was transferred to private ownership until Bigelow Tea Company bought the site, continuing Charleston's unique tea heritage. In 1995, the South Carolina General Assembly adopted Charleston tea as the state's "Official Hospitality Beverage."

and West Indian Exposition, Charleston's own world's fair. Lasting for six months, the exposition attendance nearly reached 700,000.

In the early 20th century, the Gala Festival was an annual springtime event. This was replaced by the Azalea Festival from 1934 to 1953, featuring horse shows, parades, golf tournaments and beauty contests.

After many years without such an event, Charleston was chosen to host an arts festival as a counterpart of the Festival dei Due Mondi, held in Spoleto, Italy. With a long history of the arts and many venues available to host events, Charleston was the perfect choice for Gian Carlo Menotti, founder of the Italian festival.

Today, Spoleto Festival USA is a 17-day extravaganza of the arts hosting more than 100 performances of opera, ballet, dance, music and the visual arts. Since the first Charleston festival in 1977, Spoleto has presented more than 200 international and American premieres to the more than 80,000 who attend each year.

Beyond the many performances, Charleston becomes a large, non-stop, 17-day cocktail party. Private parties held at mansions on the Battery, cast parties going late into the night at private homes, restaurants filled to capacity – all are part of Charleston's Spoleto. One Charlestonian described Spoleto as where "*foie gras* meets collard greens."

The Boathouse restaurants present these recipes for Vidalia Onion-Smoked Salmon Dip (pg. 44), Fried Oysters with Chipolte Remoulade (pg. 47), and Fried Pimento Cheese with Sundried Cranberry Jelly (pg.45) as a tribute to Spoleto Festival USA, the ultimate cocktail party.

It's a Beautiful Garden

© West Fraser

Boathouse Cocktail Sauce
Boathouse Pimento Cheese
Vidalia Onion and Smoked Salmon Dip with Boathouse Blue Cheese Chips
Fried Pimento Cheese with Sundried Cranberry Jelly
Macaroni and Cheese
Boathouse Fried Oysters with Chipotle Remoulade
Meeting Street Crab Imperial
Pan Fried Shad Roe with Bacon, Tomatoes and Scallions
Boathouse Seafood Tower
Boathouse Mussels

SPRING RECIPES

Boathouse Seafood Pasta with Mushroom and Parmesan Cream Sauce
Boathouse Grits
Boathouse Breading Mix
Pan Fried Mountain Trout with Pecan Brown Butter
Stone Crab Claws with Key Lime Dijon Mustard Dipping Sauce
Vidalia Onion Crusted Salmon with Boathouse Charred Tomato Vinaigrette and Mushroom Grits
Pecan Crusted Chicken with Maple Mustard Q
Maple Mustard Q
Boathouse Crab Cakes
Berry Shortcake with Buttermilk Ice Cream
Boathouse Key Lime Pie

Boathouse Cocktail Sauce
Makes 1 quart

With the plethora of fresh seafood available, a great cocktail sauce is a must. This sauce has been our standard and a signature recipe since the opening of the first Boathouse restaurant. Shun the store brands and make your own!

1 1/2 cups ketchup
1 1/2 cups chili sauce
2 lemons, juiced
2 teaspoons Worcestershire sauce
1 teaspoon Tabasco sauce
1/2 cup prepared horseradish

Combine all the ingredients together and store in an air-tight container.

Boathouse Pimento Cheese
Makes 10-15 servings

Pimento cheese, the "paté of the South," is a staple for picnics and boating trips. Show me a horserace without a pimento cheese sandwich or dip, and I'll show you a horserace up North.

1 pound cream cheese, softened at room temperature
4 cups mayonnaise (Duke's)
5 cups white cheddar cheese, shredded
5 cups yellow cheddar cheese, shredded
1 14-ounce can diced pimentos (liquid drained)
1 tablespoon granulated garlic
2 tablespoons paprika
2 teaspoons Tabasco sauce
2 teaspoons Worcestershire sauce
1/4 cup dill pickle juice

Combine all ingredients in a mixer and mix on low until well incorporated, or mix well in a large bowl by hand.

Vidalia Onion and Smoked Salmon Dip With Boathouse Blue Cheese Chips
Serves 8-10

This enticing dip will be a hit with your guests. Sweet onions are harvested in the spring and that alone is reason to celebrate. The most commonly known sweet onion is from Vidalia, Georgia, but the first sweets to hit to market in the spring are Texas Springsweets and Texas 1015s in March. In April, Vidalias are ready, as are Wadmalaw Sweets, grown just outside of Charleston on Wadmalaw Island.

4 tablespoons olive oil
2 medium sized Vidalia onions, sliced
2 cloves garlic, minced
2 teaspoons fresh thyme, chopped
2 tablespoons sherry vinegar
2 pounds cream cheese
1 cup parmesan cheese, softened
1 tablespoon fresh dill, chopped
2 lemons, juiced
1/2 cup sour cream
3/4 pound Boathouse smoked salmon, flaked (pg. 150)
Salt and fresh-ground black pepper
Boathouse Blue Cheese Chips (pg. 178)

In a large skillet, heat the olive oil and sauté the Vidalia onions with the garlic until lightly brown. Add the fresh thyme and sherry vinegar. Remove from heat and place the onion mixture in a mixing bowl to cool. Add the cream cheese, parmesan cheese, dill, lemon juice, and sour cream, then mix well. Lastly, gently fold in the smoked salmon. Be careful not break up the salmon chunks too much. Season the mixture with salt and fresh-ground black pepper. Serve with Boathouse Blue Cheese Chips.

44

Fried Pimento Cheese with Sundried Cranberry Jelly
Serves 8-10

Proving that pimento cheese is not just for sandwiches and dips, this creative recipe will be a hit at your cocktail party or as an hors d'ouevre.

Sundried Cranberry Jelly:
1 cup raspberry vinegar
1 cup red wine vinegar
2 cups brown sugar
1 cup sundried cranberries
1 tablespoon Tabasco sauce
1 red bell pepper, diced

Combine the vinegars and sugar in a small pot and bring to a simmer. Cook for 5 minutes and add the cranberries, Tabasco and bell pepper. Continue to cook for 30 minutes until vinegar begins to reduce and mixture thickens to a syrupy consistency.

FOR THE PIMENTO CHEESE:
3 cups Boathouse Pimento Cheese (pg. 44)
1 cup flour
3 eggs, beaten with 1/4 cup water
2 cups panko bread crumbs, pulsed in a food processor
3 cups peanut or canola oil for frying
2 cups cranberry jelly

Using a small ice cream scoop, portion the pimento cheese into balls. Roll them in flour, then in the egg mixture and, finally, in the panko crumbs. Lay the breaded cheese on a baking sheet, place in the freezer and allow them to freeze solid. While cheese hardens, heat the peanut oil in a large pot to 350 degrees. Once the cheese is hardened, drop one by one into the oil, being careful not to overcrowd. Fry the cheese for 3 to 5 minutes. Place on top of cranberry jelly and serve immediately.

CHEF'S NOTE:
Adding too much cheese at one time will rapidly lower the temperature of the oil, resulting in an oily and soggy product. This rule of thumb is applicable anytime you fry.

45

Macaroni and Cheese
Serves 4-6

Macaroni and cheese is as southern as boiled peanuts and sweet tea (Does it come any other way?). While a simple dish, follow this recipe to make a hit at the family picnic or for Sunday dinner.

2 cups half and half
1/2 pound cream cheese
1 teaspoon minced garlic
1 cup grated sharp cheddar cheese
1 cup grated parmesan cheese
2 teaspoons salt
1/4 teaspoon fresh-ground black pepper
1/4 teaspoon Tabasco sauce
1 pound cooked elbow macaroni
1 cup bread crumbs
1 1/2 tablespoons butter, melted

Preheat the oven to 400 degrees. In a sauce pot, combine the half and half, garlic and cream cheese together, then bring to a simmer. While stirring, add the cheddar and parmesan cheese, then remove from the heat. Puree the sauce until smooth and then combine with the cooked macaroni. Add the salt, fresh-ground black pepper and Tabasco. Pour into a greased casserole dish and sprinkle with bread crumbs. Drizzle with the melted butter and bake for 20 minutes until golden brown and bubbly.

CHEF'S NOTE:
This recipe also allows for individual preparations. Many varieties of cheese can be used.

Boathouse Fried Oysters with Chipotle Remoulade
Serves 8

Fried oysters are much beloved, but adding the chipotle remoulade dip sets this dish apart.

FOR THE CHIPOTLE REMOULADE:
2 each chipotles, packed in adobo sauce,
   pureed in food processor
4 cups mayonnaise (Duke's works the best,
   a Southern favorite!)
1/4 teaspoon Tabasco brand green pepper sauce
1/4 teaspoon red Tabasco sauce
1 lime, juiced

Combine all ingredients and mix well.

FOR THE OYSTERS:
3 cups peanut or canola oil
40 oysters, shucked or by the quart,
   packed in their own juice
3 cups Boathouse Breading Mix (pg. 51)
2 cups buttermilk

In a medium sauce pot, heat the peanut or canola oil to 350 degrees. While the oil heats, drain the oysters very well and place in a bowl. Cover the oysters with the buttermilk. One by one, lightly coat the oysters by dipping them in the breading mix. Once all of the oysters have been breaded, drop them into the hot oil 10 at a time; do not overcrowd them. Remove the oysters with a wire skimmer or a slotted spoon and drain on paper towel-lined plates. Serve immediately with chipotle remoulade.

47

Meeting Street Crab Imperial
Serves 8-10 as a side dish

The recipes for Meeting Street Crab and Crab Imperial are very similar, so we decided to combine them to make a Boathouse "original." We also use this recipe with oysters, which we broil on the half shell, or with steaks for a twist on surf and turf.

1 tablespoon butter
1 tablespoon flour
1/2 cup milk
1/4 cup heavy cream
1 tablespoon sherry
1/4 teaspoon salt
1/4 teaspoon white pepper
1/2 teaspoon lemon juice
1/8 teaspoon Tabasco sauce
1/8 teaspoon Worcestershire sauce
1/2 cup Duke's mayonnaise
1 pound crab meat, jumbo lump or lump
4 tablespoons chopped parsley
1/2 tablespoon Hungarian paprika
1 cup bread crumbs
1 cup grated sharp cheese, such as cheddar or gruyere
1/4 cup melted butter

Preheat oven to 400 degrees. In a small sauce pot, melt the butter, then whisk in the flour, cooking for 5 minutes. Add the milk and cream. While stirring, cook sauce until it starts to thicken, about 3 to 5 minutes. Add the sherry, pepper, lemon juice, Tabasco and Worcestershire, then cook for 2 more minutes. Remove the pan, place mixture in a bowl and set aside to cool. Once cool, whisk in the mayonnaise. Next, gently fold in the crabmeat, careful not to break up the lumps. Fold in the parsley.

Lightly grease a casserole dish. Add the crab mixture to the dish and top with bread crumbs, cheese, paprika and drizzle with the melted butter. Bake the casserole for 15-20 minutes until bubbly and golden brown.

Pan Fried Shad Roe with Bacon, Tomatoes and Scallions
Serves 6

Here's a dinner worth driving an hour to enjoy. Shad roe recipes with bacon abound, but the addition of the tomato scallion sauce finishes this dish nicely.

6 pieces shad roe
Salt and fresh-ground black pepper
Flour for dusting, about 1 cup
2 tablespoons canola oil
1/2 cup slab bacon, diced
1/2 tablespoon chopped garlic
1 cup chopped plum tomatoes
1/2 cup chopped scallions
1/4 cup stock, chicken or fish
   (canned clam juice works well)
1 tablespoon butter
6 cups cooked Boathouse grits (pg. 51)

Season the shad roe with salt and fresh-ground black pepper. Lightly coat the seasoned roe with flour, shaking off the excess. In a large skillet over medium heat, render the bacon in the canola oil until bacon is slightly crispy. With a slotted spoon, remove the bacon pieces for later use, then reserve the bacon grease and oil in the pan.

Over medium heat, cook the shad roe in the bacon grease for 3 to 5 minutes or until golden brown. Turn over and cook another 3 to 5 minutes. Remove the shad roe from the skillet and keep warm in 200 degree oven on a paper towel-lined plate. In the same skillet, add the garlic and sauté for 1 minute. Add the tomatoes, scallions and partially cooked bacon, sautéing for 5 more minutes. Add the stock and bring to a simmer. Remove from heat and whisk in the butter to make a sauce. To serve, place cooked shad roe on top of the grits and pour the bacon-tomato sauce over the top.

48

Boathouse Seafood Tower
Serves 10

At the Boathouse, we believe the best preparation for great food is fresh and simple. This dish embodies our restaurant's mission statement: "Simply fresh seafood." The seafood tower always makes a great impression. Enjoy the bounty from the sea with your choice of sauce accompaniment.

2 dozen Carolina Cup or Gulf oysters, shucked
2 dozen Breach Inlet Topneck clams, shucked
2 pounds steamed king crab legs, shells cracked
2 pounds pickled shrimp (pg. 108)
1 cup chipotle remoulade (pg. 47)
2 cups Boathouse cocktail sauce (pg. 44)
1 recipe red wine mignonette (pg. 150)
Lots of lemon wedges

Set the oysters and clams on a bed of crushed ice. Surround with the king crab legs. Set the bowl of pickled shrimp in the middle of the platter. Place the chipotle remoulade, cocktail sauce and mignonette on the side, then serve with lemon wedges.

Boathouse Mussels
Serves 8

Native Americans used mussels for food, tools and jewelry. From 1890 until plastics were invented in the 1950s, mussel shells were used to make buttons. Fortunately for us, they are also for eating. Though less popular than other shellfish, mussels cooked in a wine-saffron broth make a tempting dish.

3 tablespoons olive oil
4 pounds mussels, rinsed and cleaned
1 shallot, minced
1 clove garlic, minced
1/4 cup white wine
1 1/2 cups saffron broth (pg. 113)
1 teaspoon chopped parsley
1/2 teaspoon chopped basil
1/2 teaspoon chopped chives
3 plum tomatoes, chopped
2 tablespoons butter, softened
Salt and fresh-ground black pepper

In a large skillet with lid, heat the olive oil until it just begins to smoke. Add the mussels, shallots and garlic, then sauté for 1 minute. Add the white wine, saffron broth, all the herbs, tomatoes and butter. Cover and let the mussels steam for 4 more minutes. Season with salt and fresh-ground black pepper and serve immediately.

50

Boathouse Seafood Pasta with Mushroom and Parmesan Cream Sauce
Serves 6

Pasta dishes found their way into Charleston recipe books by the 19th century. Here, the Boathouse chefs offer a delicious seafood pasta served with mushrooms and a parmesan cream sauce.

4 tablespoons vegetable or canola oil
20 medium shrimp, peeled and deveined
20 medium sea scallops, cleaned and foot removed
1 1/2 pounds assorted fresh fish cut into 1-inch cubes
    (grouper, salmon or mahi-mahi)
1 tablespoon minced garlic
1 shallot, minced
1 cup assorted sliced mushrooms such as cremini, shiitake
    or portabella
1/4 cup white wine
2 cups heavy cream
2 teaspoons chopped Italian parsley
1 teaspoon chopped fresh basil
1 teaspoon minced fresh chives
1/2 cup parmesan cheese, grated
1 pound linguine

In a large skillet, heat the oil over medium heat until it starts smoking. Add the shrimp, scallops and cubed fresh fish and cook for 2 minutes. Add the garlic, shallots and mushrooms, and continue cooking for 2 to 3 more minutes. Add the white wine to deglaze, and reduce by half. Add heavy cream. Allow cream to reduce until it reaches syrupy consistency, about 3 minutes. Finish with the basil, chives and parmesan cheese. Serve over cooked linguine and garnish with fresh chopped parsley.

Boathouse Grits
Yields 5 cups

Lowcountry food all starts here. Without a solid grits recipe, you don't have a chance in the Carolinas. The secret is long cooking time over low heat. No self-respecting southerner would stake his family name on "instant grits."

2 cups milk
1 cup water
1 cup half and half
1/4 pound butter
3/4 cup Boathouse Stone Ground Grits (pg. 178)
Salt and fresh-ground black pepper

Place the milk, water, half and half and butter in sauce pot over medium heat and bring to a simmer. Reduce heat to low, and slowly whisk the grits into the liquid. Continue to cook on low heat for 1 1/2 to 2 hours, stirring frequently. Season with salt and fresh-ground black pepper.

51

Boathouse Breading Mix
Makes 1 1/2 quarts

1 pound seafood breader
1 pound Japanese style bread crumbs (panko)

Grind the panko in a food processor to a coarse powder consistency. Mix thoroughly with the seafood breader.

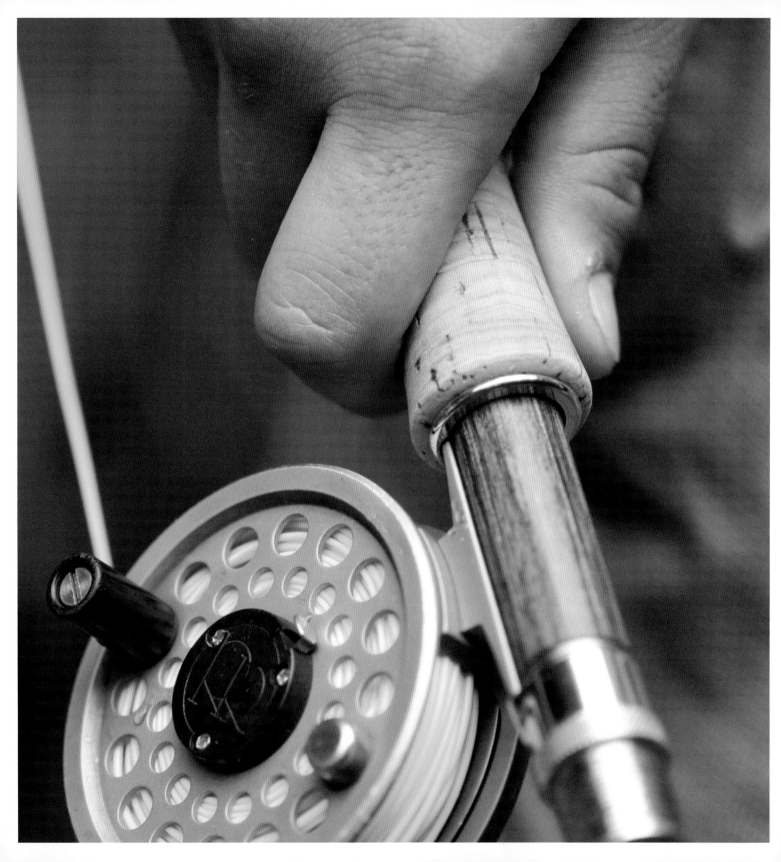

Pan Fried Mountain Trout with Pecan Brown Butter
Serves 4

As soon as the water begins to warm in the mountains, the trout begin to move. Reward yourself after a day of fishing with this trout finished off with pecan brown butter.

8 filets of rainbow trout
Salt and fresh-ground black pepper
Flour for dusting, about 1/2 cup
4 tablespoons vegetable or canola oil
3 tablespoons butter, cubed
1/2 cup coarsely chopped pecans
Juice of 1 lemon
2 tablespoons chopped parsley

Season trout with salt and pepper. Using the flour, lightly coat the trout, shaking off the excess. In a large skillet, heat the oil and 1 tablespoon of the butter. When butter starts to foam, add the trout and cook for 5 to 7 minutes, skin side up. Turn trout over and continue cooking on the other side, another 5 to 7 minutes. Remove the trout from pan and keep warm. Pour off any residual oil and return pan to heat.

Add the remaining 2 tablespoons of butter. Swirl around until the butter starts to foam, turns a light golden brown color and smells nutty. Remove pan from heat. Add the pecans and lemon juice off the heat and swirl around to lightly toast the pecans. Immediately pour sauce over the fish and sprinkle with chopped parsley.

Stone Crab Claws with Key Lime Dijon Mustard Dipping Sauce
Serves 6-8

Stone crabs are found in the coastal waters from North Carolina to Mexico, though most people think of stone crab claws as a Florida product. These crabs are harvested in South Carolina, as elsewhere, for their claws. When captured, only the largest of the two claws may be taken before the crab is turned loose. Stone crabs can regenerate their lost claws as many as four times in their lives. They are usually found near oyster reefs, feeding on oysters and blue crabs. Our stone crab claws are supplied by local legends Toby Van Buren and Bill Fennell. We tip our hats to our Florida neighbors with the choice of a Key Lime Dijon Mustard Dipping Sauce.

2 to 3 pounds fresh stone crab claws,
   steamed and cracked
1 cup whole grain Dijon mustard
1/2 cup key lime juice (Nellie & Joe's)
2 tablespoons champagne vinegar
1/4 cup mayonnaise
2 to 3 lemons, cut into wedges
Lettuce or spinach for garnish

Combine the mustard, key lime juice, vinegar and mayo together in a small bowl then whisk until smooth. Present the crab claws on a bed of lettuce and serve with the sauce on the side.

53

Vidalia Onion Crusted Salmon with Boathouse Charred Tomato Vinaigrette and Mushroom Grits

Serves 6

Grits are a foundation for many a great meal. The vinaigrette in this dish can be used on all varieties of grilled fish and meats with great results.

FOR THE GRITS:
2 cups milk
2 cups half and half
1/4 pound plus 2 tablespoons butter
3/4 cup stone ground grits
4 tablespoons olive oil
2 teaspoons chopped fresh thyme
2 cups assorted mushrooms (cremini, shiitake, portabella, hedgehog, chanterelle or whatever you can find)
2 shallots, minced
1 garlic clove, minced
Salt and fresh-ground black pepper

Start this dish by making the grits. In a medium sauce pot, heat the milk, 1/4 pound butter and the half and half until simmering. Whisk in the grits and cook for 30 minutes on low heat, stirring frequently.

While the grits are cooking, heat a large skillet. Add the olive oil and 2 tablespoons of butter. When the butter begins to foam, add the thyme, mushrooms, garlic and shallots. Cook mushrooms on medium heat until golden and slightly crispy, about 5 to 8 minutes. Remove pan from heat and add mushrooms to the grits.

FOR THE BOATHOUSE VINAIGRETTE:
4 to 5 plum tomatoes, cut in half
1 large onion, sliced into thick rings
Oil for brushing
1/2 cup balsamic vinegar
1/2 cup rice wine vinegar
3 cloves garlic, minced
2 cups olive oil
2 tablespoons chopped parsley
2 tablespoons chopped basil
Salt and fresh-ground black pepper

Heat the grill on high or heat a large skillet until blazing hot. Lightly coat the tomatoes and onion rings with oil and char them on the grill or in the skillet. This process will take about 5 to 8 minutes on the grill or 3 to 4 minutes in the skillet. Remove tomatoes and onions from the grill or skillet to cool.

Once cool, chop roughly and place in a food processor. Add the balsamic vinegar, rice wine vinegar and garlic. While blending the mixture, slowly drizzle in the olive oil to emulsify the vinaigrette. Finally, add the herbs and season with salt and pepper.

FOR THE SALMON:
2 large Vidalia onions, sliced very thin on a mandolin
1 egg
1/2 cup all purpose flour
Salt and fresh-ground black pepper
6 6-ounce filets of salmon, skin removed
4 tablespoons oil (canola or vegetable)
6 sprigs fresh thyme

To finish the dish, mix the sliced Vidalia onions with the egg and flour. Season the salmon filets with salt and pepper. Smear filets with the onion mixture. Heat a large skillet with oil over medium heat. Add salmon with the onion, crust facing down. Cook salmon until the crust is golden brown, about 4 minutes. Turn over salmon and continue cooking for another 4 to 6 minutes for medium. If you prefer your salmon fully cooked, place in a 350-degree oven for an additional 4 to 6 minutes. Remove from pan and allow salmon to rest for 5 to 8 minutes. Place on top of the grits and drizzle the tomato vinaigrette around the side. Garnish with fresh thyme sprigs.

Pecan Crusted Chicken with Maple Mustard Q

Serves 6

Serve this chicken with our "best ever" collards and smoked gouda macaroni and cheese for a delicious dinner.

FOR THE PECAN CRUST:
1 cup chopped pecans
1 cup Panko (Japanese) bread crumbs
2 cups flour

Chop the pecans with the bread crumbs in a food processor until fine. Add the flour and mix. Pour the pecan mixture in a medium bowl.

6 8-ounce chicken breasts, trimmed of fat, lobes separated and pounded lightly
2 cups buttermilk
Salt and fresh-ground black pepper
5 cups peanut or vegetable oil for frying
1/2 cup Maple Mustard Q

In a shallow container, cover the chicken with buttermilk and season with salt and fresh-ground black pepper, soaking for 2 hours.

In a large pot, heat vegetable oil to 350 degrees. Remove each chicken breast from buttermilk and drain excess liquid. Dredge the chicken breasts in the pecan crust until evenly coated. Carefully drop the breaded chicken in the hot oil and fry until golden brown and cooked through, about 7 to 8 minutes. Carefully remove chicken from the oil and drain on paper towel-lined plates. Serve with Maple Mustard Q.

Maple Mustard Q

Makes 1 quart

This enticing sauce is great on chicken, pork or as a glaze for shrimp. You can substitute sorghum syrup for cane syrup, honoring our mountain traditions.

2 cups maple syrup
1 cup Dijon mustard
1 cup cane syrup
1/2 cup mayonnaise

Combine the maple syrup, mustard and cane syrup in medium sauce pan, then cook for 15 minutes. Remove from heat and whisk in mayonnaise. Once smooth, set aside to cool for later use.

55

Boathouse Crab Cakes
Serves 6

Many states lay claim to crab and crab recipes. The Atlantic blue crabs caught off the Carolina coast are plentiful and delicious. As a child, there's no sport more rewarding than going crabbing. It requires less patience than fishing and produces plenty of delicious results. These crab cakes may be served individually as an appetizer or serve several as a dinner.

1 pound claw meat
1 pound lump meat
1 pound backfin or special meat
2 cups mayonnaise (Duke's)
2 teaspoons Old Bay seasoning
2 tablespoons dried parsley
1 lemon, juiced
2 eggs
1 teaspoon each salt and pepper
3 cups Japanese bread crumbs or Panko (two cups for the
   mixture, one cup for coating the crab cakes)
4 tablespoons canola or vegetable oil
1 cup Boathouse Green Tabasco Cream Sauce (pg. 178)

Thoroughly pick the crab meat to remove any hard parts. In a bowl, combine the mayonnaise, Old Bay, parsley, lemon juice, eggs, salt and pepper and whisk until smooth. Add crabmeat and gently mix to incorporate all the crab into the mayonnaise mixture. Mix in the 2 cups of bread crumbs and refrigerate for 30 minutes. This gives the bread crumbs time to absorb.

Form the crab cake mixture into 4 ounce or 1/2 cup cakes. Roll the cakes in the reserved 1 cup of bread crumbs.

To cook the crab cakes, heat oil over medium heat in cast iron or fry pan. Place cakes into pan and sear until golden brown; turn over and repeat on other side.

Serve over warmed Boathouse Green Tabasco Cream Sauce and garnish with fresh minced chives.

56

Berry Shortcake
With Buttermilk Ice Cream
Serves 8

Early spring strawberries prepared with this recipe are a rare treat. You can substitute blackberries, blueberries and raspberries in season during late spring and summer. Peaches are also a great alternative.

FOR THE ICE CREAM:
4 cups buttermilk
1/2 cup sugar
2 lemons, zest and juice
1 teaspoon vanilla extract

Combine the ingredients and churn in an ice cream maker, following the manufacturer's directions.

FOR THE BISCUITS:
2 cups all purpose flour
5 tablespoons sugar
1 tablespoon baking powder
1 teaspoon salt
8 tablespoons butter, chilled, cut into cubes
1/2 cup plus 2 tablespoons cream

To prepare the biscuits, preheat oven to 450 degrees.

In a bowl, combine the flour, sugar, baking powder and salt. Work the butter by hand into the flour until it becomes mealy. Stir in 1/2 cup cream, working just enough so that a dough forms. Do not knead. Roll out the dough to about 1-inch thickness on floured surface. Cut the biscuits using a 2 1/2 inch round biscuit cutter. Brush the biscuits with the remaining 2 tablespoons of cream and place on a parchment-lined baking sheet or lightly greased pan and

bake for 10 minutes. Reduce the heat to 325 degrees and bake until golden, about 10 minutes. Cool before slicing in half.

FRUIT:
10 cups berries (strawberries work best)
6 tablespoons sugar

Combine the berries with the sugar and let stand for 20 to 30 minutes. To serve, lay half a biscuit on a plate. Place 1 scoop of buttermilk ice cream on top. Spoon berries over and top with remaining biscuit, then top with whipped cream.

FOR THE WHIPPED CREAM:
2 cups heavy cream
1/4 cup powdered sugar

Mix both ingredients with handheld electric mixer or stand mixer until cream reaches medium stiff peaks.

59

Add a lump of butter the size of an egg. Beat the eggs while you sing two stanzas of a hymn.

– Cooking instructions in an Appalachian recipe

Boathouse Key Lime Pie
Serves 8-10

The official dessert of Key West, Florida, is now a Southern standard. You just don't get any more Southern than Key West, literally. Our deep south neighbors were challenged by being so remote; milk deliveries, before the railroad reached Key West in 1912, were infrequent. This simple dessert was created after Gail Borden's invention of sweetened condensed (canned) milk in 1859. The limes were already there. Don't even think of making this without Nellie and Joe's Lime Juice from, of course, Key West.

FOR THE CRUST:
1 1/2 cups graham cracker crumbs
4 ounces light brown sugar
4 ounces whole unsalted butter

Preheat oven to 350 degrees.

In a small sauce pan, melt the butter over low heat. In a mixing bowl combine the graham cracker crumbs with the brown sugar. Pour butter over the brown sugar and crumbs and mix thoroughly. Spray a 9-inch pie pan with non-stick spray. Pour crumb mixture into pie pan and press mixture against the bottom and sides in one even layer. Place pie crust in oven for 5 to 7 minutes to pre-bake crust. Remove from oven and cool to room temperature.

FOR THE PIE FILLING:
5 whole eggs
6 ounces key lime juice
1 1/2 cups sweetened condensed milk
1 teaspoon salt

Whisk together the eggs, condensed milk and salt. While whisking, slowly pour in the key lime juice until thoroughly incorporated. Pour mixture into pie crust. Bake in 350-degree oven for 15 to 20 minutes or until center is firm. Remove from oven and let cool to room temperature before slicing.

To keep artichokes all the year, put them in a barl and lay every layer with sand that the leaves do not touch one another. Then bury about a foot into the ground.

– Eliza Lucas Pinckney, 1756

OKRA
$1. 49

SHEM CREEK CHARTERS

CAROLINA CLIPPER

SUMMER

Summer is a time of plenty along the coast and in the mountains. Tomatoes, squash, beans, corn, cucumbers and greens are all in season. In the mountains, summer crops were critical. Not only did they provide sustenance and enough food to put up for the winter, but they also produced a surplus to sell. While the coastal farmers frequently enjoyed two growing seasons, the mountains offered only one to prepare for the challenges of winter.

Once the Buncombe Turnpike was open, travel to the mountains for Charlestonians was possible; but, in the 19th century, it was still a two-week trip. The Civil War interrupted any thought of immediately extending the railroad to the Blue Ridge; by the 1870s, however, plans were under way once more.

Railroad investors identified three possible routes to connect Spartanburg, South Carolina, to Asheville, North Carolina. Routes through Howard's Gap and Tryon Mountain were possible, but the distance was excessive. The most direct route was over Pace's Gap through today's town of Saluda. Shorter and cheaper than its alternatives, this run became the steepest grade in the United States for a standard gauge mainline track. From Melrose to Saluda, a distance of three miles, the grade increases almost 900 feet.

While only three miles "as the crow flies," the curvature in the track to make this grade possible resulted in a 12-mile stretch. The elevation between mileposts 113 and 122 was 891.5 feet. On July 4, 1878, the first passenger train made it up the Saluda Grade. By the following summer, the rail line was complete to Hendersonville, reaching Asheville in December 1885.

Many wrecks occurred when trains "slipped" on the track going up the mountain or built up too much speed going down. The treacherous sharp turns descending the mountain earned nicknames such as "Slaughter Pen Cut." The train itself was named the "Carolina Special" but aptly nicknamed "The Carolina Creeper" to honor the difficult ascent.

Finally, a "helper" locomotive was added to the back of the train in Melrose to push the train up the mountain, disconnecting after the arduous climb. On the trip back down the mountain, the second engine was added once again to hold the train back. Many mountain residents and "summer people" have fond memories of hearing the train whistles through the Blue Ridge.

In the 20th century, it became customary for many Charleston families to spend summers in the mountains – the head of the household typically visited on the weekends. Businessmen referred to the end-of-the-week train trip to the mountains as "the world's longest cocktail party."

In the 18th and 19th centuries, those Lowcountry residents who could, escaped Charleston to avoid the scourge of malaria. By the 20th century, the annual pilgrimage to the mountains was primarily social in nature. The old family mountain homes and the allure of the cool, fresh air of the Blue Ridge Mountains continued to attract Charlestonians. The Charleston *News and Courier* published the temperature readings in Charleston and Flat Rock side by side.

Two notable Charlestonians were among the summer people: DuBose Heyward, author of Porgy and collaborator with George Gershwin in the great American opera *Porgy and Bess*, maintained a summer residence in Flat Rock, as did Mary Middleton Pinckney Lee,

64

The family was supplied with every kind of vegetable. I have never forgotten the large dishes of figs, plums, watermelon and muskmelon.

– Rose Ravenel speaking of the family farm in St. Andrews Parish, 1860 the widow of Robert E. Lee III. "Rock Hill," the mountain estate built by Christopher Memminger in 1839, was sold and became home to noted author and historian Carl Sandburg. Renamed "Connemara," the Sandburg home is today a National Park Service site.

Once Interstate-26 was completed from Charleston to the North Carolina state line, the need for and interest in the Carolina Creeper faded. The last passenger train made its way up the treacherous Saluda Grade in November 1968. The quick and direct highway route to the mountains reduced the trek to Flat Rock by six hours.

In Charleston, the month of June is ideal for shark fishing as the shark move in to feed on bluefish. By late June, offshore fishing produces marlin, tuna, dolphin and wahoo. Near-shore fishing yields bluefish, king and Spanish mackerel. Inshore, the warm waters produce ample opportunities to catch croaker, spot and sea bass. Summer is also the season to gig for flounder. The coastal waters provided bountiful catches for the men of the Mosquito Fleet to sell in Charleston.

Another summertime sport is crabbing. Most every dock has a crab trap or two hung over the side. In the tidal rivers, children wade out thigh-deep to drop a chicken neck with a fishing weight tied to a string in the water while balancing a long-handled dip net in the other hand, waiting to scoop up the clawed scavenger.

Of course, summer is the time for fresh fruits. Carolina peach season runs from mid-June to mid-August. Early Charleston families enjoyed peaches in every way imaginable, from fresh peaches to peach leather, pickled peaches, peach butter, peach tree tea and peach brandy.

Figs were brought to Carolina by the Spanish in the 16th century; the summer delicacy was awaiting English colonists when Charleston was settled in the 1670s. On the coast, many families had a couple of fig trees in the backyard. By late July and August, Charlestonians daily partook of the early morning ritual of harvesting the ripening figs before the birds could feast on them.

Tomato Sandwiches

Whether grown in your own garden or purchased from one of many produce stands that dot the rural roadways, the first fresh, vine-ripe tomato of the season is cause for celebration. Many Charlestonians dedicate frequent meals, lunch and dinner, to the very simple but delicious tomato sandwich.

Given the few ingredients that comprise a tomato sandwich, variations would seem limited. But consider the myriad choices – kind of bread, brand of mayonnaise, spicing, to peel or not to peel, and tomato varietals. Here's the process for the "classic" Lowcountry tomato sandwich:

> *1 juicy, red, vine-ripe tomato (preferably from John's Island or Wadmalaw Island)*
> *Duke's Mayonnaise*
> *White bread*
> *Salt and pepper*

Carefully select the vine-ripe tomato (best from the farmer's market or a roadside stand, unless, of course, you grow your own). Peel the tomato skin carefully. Slice the tomato and lay flat. Apply salt and pepper to taste. Apply mayonnaise generously to 2 slices of bread and add the prepared tomato slice.

Caution: Eating could be messy and habit-forming.

Chef's note: If only store-bought tomatoes are available, DO NOT attempt to prepare this sandwich – wait for another day.

In late summer, the much-maligned vegetable – okra – reaches maturity. Brought from West Africa, okra had entered North America through the slave trade in Charleston by the early 18th century. The African word for okra is "gombo," yielding the American word "gumbo" to refer to various soups with seasonal vegetables. Charleston okra soup (pg. 86) has graced Lowcountry tables for centuries. For those not up to the "ooze" of okra, try it fried (pg. 86). During the Civil War, when regular rations were short or supplies could not make their way through the blockades, okra was dried, roasted and ground as a coffee substitute. Advice: pass up the "coffee," stick to the ooze of gumbo or fry the stuff.

Another favorite, whether on the coast or in the mountains, is frog legs. Once described as a "swamp-man's lobster," frog legs, sautéed with lemon, salt and pepper, are a delicacy enjoyed for generations. Longtime Flat Rock resident Louise Howe Bailey, who descends from a Charleston family, recalls her father heading out on many a late-night adventure gigging frogs. Hunts for the large bullfrogs are best at night when they gather to feed. Their loud croaking is effective radar to locate the prized bullfrogs. Dr. Howe, armed with a gig and a flashlight, would return home with a bag full of large frogs. Bailey described the fascination of a child watching the frog legs jump, as if still alive, while being fried or sautéed – a phenomena caused by twitching leg muscles.

Of course, the most important crop for any part of the year is corn, cultivated from the coast to the mountains. Dried corn is ground into grits and cornmeal, the foundation of many Charleston recipes. In the mountains, corn was more than food. The corn shucks were used to make chair bottoms and feed animals. Corn husks were fashioned into hats, mats and horse collars.

In the mountains, corn played another important role – can't make moonshine without it. Originating with Scot-Irish settlers, moonshine has existed in the Blue Ridge Mountains for more than 250 years. Scots had been distilling whiskey as early

Sex is good, but not as good as fresh, sweet corn.

– Garrison Keillor

THE BOATHOUSE *Tales and Recipes from a Southern Kitchen*

Grits or Hominy?

Early Carolina colonists quickly learned to appreciate the value of corn, referred to by the Cherokee as, "Mother corn – giver of life." Throughout history, corn has earned the distinction of being the South's most important food.

For centuries, every community had a grist mill available to the farmers or plantations to process their corn. Today in the South, grits are produced by grinding the corn. Hominy is produced by soaking the dried corn in an alkali solution to remove the husk. In Charleston, however, cooked grits are still referred to as hominy.

A simple poem from the Junior League of Charleston's *Charleston Receipts* is most instructive.

Never call it 'Hominy Grits'
Or you will give Charlestonians fits!
When corn comes from the mill, it's grist;
After you cook it well, I wist,
You serve 'hominy!' Do not skimp;
Serve butter with it and lots of shrimp.

Do yourself a favor, pass up the grocery store instant grits and look for whole grain stone-ground or water-ground grits. The taste and quality difference is astonishing.

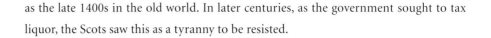

Peach Leather

Man has enjoyed sun-dried fruits since the days of ancient Egypt. While many fruits are suited for drying, peach leather has long been a Charleston favorite. Sara Rutledge, in her book, *Carolina Housewife*, offers the simple process used for centuries.

Take a peck or two of soft free-stone peaches, peel and mash them. Press the pulp through a course sieve and to 4 quarts of pulp add 1 quart of good brown sugar. Mix well together and boil for 2 minutes. Spread the paste on plates and put them in the sun every day until the cakes look dry and will leave the plates readily when a knife is passed around the edges of the cakes. Sprinkle some white sugar over the rough side and roll them up like sweet wafers. If the weather is fine, three days will be enough to dry them.

as the late 1400s in the old world. In later centuries, as the government sought to tax liquor, the Scots saw this as a tyranny to be resisted.

As the Scot-Irish arrived in the western North Carolina mountains, they brought their distilling skills with them. The rough terrain and climate was not conducive to growing the wheat they traditionally used to distill scotch whiskey, but they quickly found that corn could be distilled into a pure liquor. All liquor was untaxed up to 1791 and again from 1802 to 1862.

After the Civil War, when liquor was taxed, the distilleries went "underground." The term "moonshiner" was used to label these men who defied government tax policy. Moonshine and moonshiner come from 18th-century England, when European brandy was smuggled across the English Channel during the night. These smugglers were referred to as "moonlighters." Later in the United States, the term became "moonshiners." In the 20th century, 90 percent of all illegal liquor distilleries were in the southeast.

Corn liquor permeated the culture from the mountains to the Lowcountry: Many a pint found its way to Charleston "blind tigers" in the early 20th century. The traditional Asheville recipe for party punch included corn liquor. On a visit to the Grove Park Inn in Asheville, Henry Ford was proudly presented a jar of moonshine.

In addition to corn liquor, mountain entrepreneurs distilled fruit brandies using apples, peaches, prunes or grapes. One popular liquor was "crazy apple," a mixture of corn whiskey and apple brandy. A favorite drink of the "summer people" was cherry bounce, a concoction of corn whiskey with a dash of cherry juice and sourwood honey. Many Charleston men returned home on Mondays aboard the Carolina Creeper packing cases of corn liquor or cherry bounce. Legend has it that many early stock car racers first honed their skills as whiskey haulers determined to outrun "revenuers."

For many mountain residents, moonshining was a way to supplement their farming income. Beyond serving as a potent libation, corn liquor was also used for centuries to treat colds and pneumonia. Though it likely offered scant curative value, pixilated was a more palatable way to be "under the weather."

THE BOATHOUSE *Tales and Recipes from a Southern Kitchen*

By the summer, horse racing gave way to regattas. Like the modern horse races, the actual sport is an excuse for the social opportunities presented by the event. The Carolina Yacht Club was chartered in 1888, the first in the Lowcountry. Other clubs were founded, and boat races soon dominated the harbor during summer.

At Rockville, just south of Charleston and home to the Sea Island Yacht Club, races started in 1890 with competition between residents of Wadmalaw and Edisto islands. By 1894, a boat from James Island joined in the competition. Eventually, this regatta became a spirited competition between the sea islands (James, Johns, Wadmalaw and Edisto), Mt. Pleasant, Beaufort and Charleston. Each community built its boat, putting its best captain and crew aboard.

In 1899, James Island entered a new boat, the *Lizzie Bee*, named for the daughter of James Island Yacht Club Commodore Sandiford Stiles Bee. The new boat, captained by "Washy" Seabrook, dominated the race. Wadmalaw Island responded by building a new boat, *Undine. The Lizzie Bee, Lizzie Bee II, Undine* and *Undine II* ruled the regatta until 1912.

Many of its founding families still race at the Rockville Regatta held the first Saturday of August each year. For residents in the many boats lining Bohicket Creek during race weekend, it is the "largest party on water" of the year.

As colorful sails paint the harbor in the summer, spectators on power boats and supporters ashore enjoy the likes of cucumber-tomato salad (pg. 80), shrimp paste sandwiches (pg. 82), crab salad and blue cheese coleslaw (pg. 81).

Once the boats are in and the sun sets, Frogmore Stew is a crowd favorite. Unlike a traditional stew, Frogmore Stew is more like a seafood boil. An old and simple recipe for this crowd favorite is:

> *1 large pot of water with shrimp boil*
> * and seasoning of choice*
> *Bring to a boil.*
> *Add smoked sausage and cook (boil) for 5 minutes;*
> *Add fresh corn-on-the-cob cut into small pieces*
> * and boil for 5 minutes;*
> *Add fresh shrimp and cook for 3 minutes.*
> *Serve to a happy crowd.*

There are several variations on this "stew." Some prefer to steam the sausage, corn and shrimp. Others cook these ingredients over an open fire or on a grill. Either way, this simple dish makes a great dinner after a long day of fun.

The stew gets its name from the small town of Frogmore on St. Helena Island, near Beaufort, South Carolina. Frogmore was once a bustling seafood and caviar center, also known for harvesting diamondback turtles. In the late 20th century, the town's name was changed to St. Helena, leaving the name "Frogmore" to the cuisine and folklore of South Carolina.

Most 19th-century summer villages have disappeared. While Moultrieville no longer exists, Sullivan's Island is as busy as the mountains in the summer. Many of the people who populate the island are descendants of old Charlestonians who have forsaken the cool crisp mountain air for a constant breeze and the smell of pluff mud. Just as wives and children made the move to the mountains, these families headed to the beach. Dad worked downtown and then returned in the

71

evening. It was a comfortable existence, routine and magical at the same time.

The first notable celebration of the summer was Carolina Day on June 28, the celebration and observance of the battle of Sullivan's Island, the first victory of the Patriot cause. On June 28, 1776, an enormous British fleet with its army was impressively defeated by the small patriot force led by General William Moultrie bunkered in the not-yet-completed fortification, Fort Sullivan.

For South Carolinians, after the Civil War, June 28 was Independence Day, not the Fourth of July. In Charleston, as with many Southern communities, it took decades after the Civil War to warm to the more widely observed national holiday. The Fourth of July was viewed by Southerners as a "Yankee celebration." The day also marks the fall of Vicksburg.

While the next generation paid lip-service to the holiday, the scars of the Civil War and Charleston's federal occupation were slow to heal. By the late 1800s, Charlestonians found a renewed interest in the event, as the Spanish-American War spurred a return of national patriotism.

In the early 20th century, for those wanting to move to the beach for the summer, Sullivan's Island found a new competitor in Folly Beach. Referred to today, tongue in cheek, as "The Edge of America," Folly developed a resort atmosphere long before the establishment of Myrtle Beach and the Horry County "Grand Strand," several hours drive to the north.

Several notable Charlestonians built homes on Folly Beach including DuBose Heyward, who divided his summers between the beach and his Flat Rock home. When George Gershwin came to Charleston to collaborate with Heyward on *Porgy and Bess*, he resided at Folly Beach. Charleston artist Elizabeth O'Neill Verner and nationally recognized realist artist Edward Hopper frequently painted there. Charleston raconteur and historian Samuel Gaillard Stoney also summered on Folly.

Folly Pier, a large dance hall over the ocean, opened in 1931 and, for four decades, offered diverse musical acts from Tommy Dorsey to Hank Williams, from the Ink Spots to Doug Clark and the Hot Nuts. Many Charlestonians stole their first kiss from a summer crush shuffling on the sandy dance floor of the Pier. The Pier was lost to a great fire in 1977.

Today, Folly Beach is known for its surfing and skim-boarding devotees at "the Wash-out," actually the site of an old inlet that used to separate "Little Folly Island" from Folly Beach.

Whether on Independence Day or throughout the summer, Charlestonians summering on the beach invite their less fortunate town-bound chums for food, fellowship and celebrations. Boiled shrimp, macaroni and cheese, coleslaw and cold watermelon are the order of the day as families and friends converge at the beach.

In 1957, George Johnson, a retired brick mason and president of the Blue Ridge Coon Club, held a local barbeque in the Saluda mountains the Saturday after the Fourth of July for years. His purpose was to celebrate and raise funds to replenish the local raccoon population. Before long, the first

Coon Day Parade was held on the Fourth of July and has since defined the town. Thousands flock to Saluda, North Carolina, each year to watch the parade and enjoy the festivities.

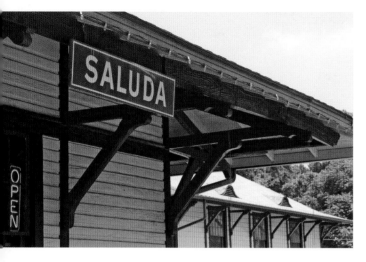

Another important tradition in the North Carolina mountains is the opening of the Flat Rock Playhouse, the State Theatre of North Carolina. In 1937, a group of performers organized a theater group, The Vagabonds. First offering eight weeks of theater in a converted grist mill, the troupe established itself in Flat Rock by 1952. The Playhouse is now open from late May through mid-October, presenting matinees and evening performances Wednesday through Sunday. The Flat Rock Playhouse hosts more than 80,000 guests per year and is considered one of the best seasonal theaters in the United States.

74

Where the young people of the region enjoyed summer 'Saint Cecilias'
– when all Flat Rock became a transplanted Charleston.

– Lawrence Brewster describing the Flat Rock Social Club

Support American Fishermen

Fish House Punch
Carrot Puree
Pineapple-Ginger Salsa
Marinated Tomatoes
Black-Eyed Pea Relish
Cucumber-Tomato Salad with Red Onion Vinaigrette
Boathouse Blue Cheese Coleslaw
Boathouse Roasted Corn and Crab Soup
Boathouse Roma Tomato Jam
Shrimp Paste Sandwiches
Jalapeno Corn Pudding

SUMMER RECIPES

Boathouse Fried Green Tomatoes
Fried Green Tomato BLT
Fried Okra with Boathouse Spicy Ranch
Charleston Okra Soup
Boathouse Steam Pot
Pan Fried Flounder with Corn-Crab Relish
Pan Roasted Carolina Wahoo with Okra, Tomato, Bacon and Fresh Corn Stew
Chipotle Black Coffee Barbecue Ribs
Salmon Cakes with Fresh Dill and Cucumbers
Peach Tart Tatin with Carolina Gold Rice Pudding & Shrewsberry Cookies
"Free Form" Peach Pie

Fish House Punch

Makes 4 gallons

This is a wonderful summer garden party punch.

3 cups lemon juice
1 cup simple syrup
6 cups brandy
2 cups peach schnapps
2 cups light rum
2 cups strong tea
4 cups club soda
2 cups sliced fresh peaches

Mix together all ingredients except fresh peaches and chill. Pour over peaches in a glass pitcher or tall glasses to serve.

Carrot Puree

Serves 6-8

This is a great alternative to mashed potatoes and is perfect with grilled or roasted fish.

8-9 carrots, peeled and coarsely chopped
1 small Vidalia onion, chopped
1/4 cup unsalted butter
Salt and fresh-ground black pepper

Place carrots and onion in a small sauce pot and cover with water. Bring water to a boil then turn down to a simmer. Cook carrots until very tender, about 20 minutes. Drain the carrots well and place in a food processor. Puree until smooth, adding butter. Season with salt and fresh-ground black pepper.

Pineapple-Ginger Salsa

Makes 2 quarts

This recipe is great for summertime affairs. Serve with fresh grilled Mahi-Mahi (dolphin) or Yellowfin Tuna.

1 golden pineapple – peeled, cored and diced
1 small red onion, diced
1 red bell pepper, diced
1 small jalapeno, membranes and seeds
  removed and minced
1 tablespoon, grated fresh ginger
1/4 cup chopped cilantro
1 tablespoon chopped mint
1 lime, juiced
Salt and fresh-ground black pepper

Mix all ingredients together and chill 1 to 2 hours before using.

Marinated Tomatoes

Makes 1 quart

Make this dish ahead. Goes great with fresh shrimp – quick, easy and delicious.

6 to 7 plum tomatoes, cored and diced
1/2 cup Balsamic Vinegar
1/2 cup Extra Virgin Olive Oil
3 tablespoons finely shredded fresh basil
Salt and fresh-ground black pepper

Mix all ingredients together in a large bowl and chill well before serving.

78

Black-Eyed Pea Relish
Makes 2 quarts

A staple in Southern dishes for three centuries, black-eyed peas found their way to Charleston from the Caribbean. They're not just for Hoppin' John. This relish is a great accompaniment to everything from fried green tomatoes to hamburgers. Enjoy!

1/2 pound dried black-eyed peas
2 quarts water
1 red pepper, diced
1 yellow pepper, diced
1 green pepper, diced
1 yellow onion, diced
1/2 bunch cilantro, finely chopped
2 limes, juiced
2 teaspoons cumin
1 teaspoon paprika
1/4 cup rice wine vinegar
1/4 cup olive oil
Salt and pepper to taste

In a small sauce pan, cook the peas over high heat in water for 25 to 30 minutes or until fork tender. Strain peas and spread evenly onto a large plate to cool. In a medium-sized mixing bowl, whisk together the vinegar, oil, lime juice and dry spices. Add the peppers, onion and cilantro to the liquid. Finally, mix in the cooked peas and season with salt and pepper.

Cucumber-Tomato Salad with Red Onion Vinaigrette
Serves 6-8

This is a wonderfully light salad, perfect for summertime lunch or dinner. Always look for the freshest, ripest tomatoes you can find to make this refreshing salad.

4 English cucumbers, peeled and sliced thin
4 to 5 large very ripe tomatoes sliced into large pieces
2 sprigs basil, thinly sliced
1 teaspoon chopped fresh thyme
2 red onions, sliced 1/2 inch
1/2 cup balsamic vinegar
3/4 cup extra virgin olive oil
1 tablespoon brown sugar
2 garlic cloves, smashed
Salt and lots of fresh-ground black pepper

Place the cucumbers, tomatoes, basil and thyme in a large bowl and mix. Keep chilled.

Heat a large skillet until very hot. Lay the onion slices in skillet lightly and char about 2 to 3 minutes on both sides. Chop the onions roughly and place them in a small bowl. Add the balsamic vinegar, olive oil, brown sugar and garlic. Season well with salt and pepper and pour over the cucumber mixture. Toss well and serve immediately.

Boathouse Blue Cheese Coleslaw

Serves 6-8

It wouldn't be summertime in the South without coleslaw. Blue cheese coleslaw was created by our founding chef Jeff Lanzaro at the Boathouse at Breach Inlet. Acknowledging that imitation is the sincerest form of flattery, blue cheese coleslaw is now found in many restaurants. This interesting preparation complements any dish, from fish to barbeque.

1/2 cup mayonnaise (Duke's)
4 tablespoons sour cream
2 teaspoons balsamic vinegar
1/8 teaspoon cayenne pepper
1/2 cup crumbled blue cheese
1 pound white cabbage, shredded (about 6 cups)
2 medium carrots, peeled and grated
1 small red onion, diced

Combine the mayonnaise, sour cream, vinegar and cayenne pepper, mixing until smooth in a large bowl. Add the blue cheese crumbles and fold with mixture. Next, add the cabbage, carrots, red onion and mix until well incorporated.

CHEF'S NOTE:
Any sharp blue cheese (Danish, Clemson) will work for this recipe. Many Southerners prefer Duke's Mayonnaise, but any variety will do.

Boathouse Roasted Corn and Crab Soup

Serves 8

Many recipes for crab soup can be found among the historic receipt books from the Lowcountry. This rendition by the Boathouse pays homage to two staples from the coast – corn and crab. You'll delight your guests with this preparation!

1/4 pound butter
1 each red, yellow, and green bell peppers, diced
1 small yellow onion, diced
2 ribs celery, diced
1/2 pound andouille sausage
4 cloves garlic, minced fine
3 ears corn, shucked and kernels removed from cob
1/2 teaspoon dried thyme
2 teaspoons dried oregano
1 teaspoon Boathouse Blackening Seasoning (pg. 178)
1/2 cup all purpose flour
2 cups bottled clam juice or fish stock
1 cup milk
1 cup heavy cream
1/2 pound claw crabmeat, cleaned of any hard parts
Salt and fresh-ground black pepper

81

In large pot, melt butter over medium heat. When the butter starts to foam, add the bell peppers, onion, celery, andouille sausage, garlic and corn. Sauté for 5 minutes and then add the thyme, oregano and Boathouse Blackening Seasoning. Add the flour, stirring to avoid lumps. Turn to low heat and continue cooking for 5 to 7 minutes, stirring constantly. Slowly add the clam juice while stirring, so no lumps form. Simmer the soup for 5 to 7 minutes. Add the milk and cream and continue to heat until soup begins to thicken. Lower heat and let simmer for 2 to 3 minutes. Finally, add crab meat and serve.

Boathouse Roma Tomato Jam
Serves 12

This "jam" is the perfect accompaniment for any number of delicately fried vegetables such as green tomatoes, zucchini squash or okra.

1 1/2 quarts roma tomatoes, chopped
1 medium sweet onion, minced
1 cup brown sugar
1 tablespoon chopped garlic
1 cup balsamic vinegar
2 tablespoons extra virgin olive oil
Salt and fresh-ground black pepper to taste

Over medium-high heat, sauté the onions, tomatoes and garlic in the olive oil. Reduce heat to low and add the balsamic vinegar and brown sugar. Continue to cook over low heat until mixture reaches jam-like consistency, about 30 minutes. Season with salt and pepper and serve at room temperature, or refrigerate for later use.

Shrimp Paste Sandwiches
Serves 8-10

On a boat ride or a picnic, shrimp paste sandwiches are always a hit. This snack has deep roots in the culinary traditions of the Lowcountry. Creek shrimp caught on a cast net are great for shrimp paste.

1 pound cooked small shrimp (70/90 count)
1 celery rib, minced
1 small onion, minced
1/2 teaspoon dill
1/2 cup mayonnaise
1 lemon, juiced
1 tablespoon Dijon mustard
1 loaf of Pullman bread, crusts cut off and thinly sliced

Combine the shrimp, celery, onion, dill, mayo, lemon juice and Dijon mustard in a food processor and puree until smooth. Spread shrimp paste onto the sliced bread in a thin layer and serve.

82

When it comes to Frogmore Stew, every man is his own best chef, but all recipes have hot sausage, corn and shrimp in whatever amount the cook chooses, and it doesn't seem to matter to those who eat it. The common denominator of Frogmore Stew seems to be: There's never any left!

– *New York Times*, February 1986

Jalapeno Corn Pudding

Serves 6 as a side dish

Corn pudding is a heritage dish found in the mountains and on the coast to celebrate the summer's bounty. Many family recipe books record some variation. The sweeter the corn, the better the pudding. Don't be lured into making this when the first of the Florida and Mexico corn start to show up in spring – wait for fresh, local corn!

6 ears sweet corn
3 tablespoons butter
2/3 cup heavy cream
1 1/2 teaspoons salt
1/4 teaspoon fresh-ground black pepper
2 jalapenos, seeded, membranes removed and minced
2 teaspoons pure maple syrup
1 1/2 cups milk
4 eggs
2 tablespoons cornmeal

Cut the kernels off 5 of the ears of corn, scraping the cobs with the back of a knife to remove and collect all of the "milk." Grate the remaining ear of corn on the coarse side of a box grater, collecting all the juices.

Preheat oven to 350 degrees. Using 1 tablespoon of the butter, grease a baking dish. In a large skillet, melt remaining butter over medium heat. Add all the corn including its "milk." While stirring occasionally, cook the corn until it starts to thicken slightly. Add the cream, salt, pepper, jalapeno and maple syrup. Cook for 5 more minutes until thick and a spoon leaves a trail when scraped on the bottom of the pan.

Remove from heat and place in a bowl. Stir in milk, eggs and cornmeal. Pour into the baking dish. Set dish inside a larger pan and then fill the larger pan with very hot water until it comes up half way to the smaller baking dish. Cook the mixture for 20 to 25 minutes or until the center jiggles slightly when shaken. Allow pudding to rest 10 minutes before serving.

83

Boathouse Fried Green Tomatoes

Serves 6

Fried green tomatoes, if prepared properly, have a delicate and subtle quality that can stand alone in a meal served with tomato jam or as a building block in a sandwich. The secret to great preparation is never crowding your skillet or fryer! This will help to seal the freshness of the tomato.

3 very firm, large green tomatoes, cored and cut into
  1/2 inch slices
2 cups buttermilk
3 cups vegetable or peanut oil for frying
2 cups Boathouse Breading Mix (pg. 51)

Submerge the tomato slices in the buttermilk and soak for 2 hours. In a deep sauce pot, heat the oil to 350 degrees. Pull tomatoes one at a time from the buttermilk and immediately drop into breading mix. Pat tomatoes with mix until both sides are adequately covered. Carefully drop the breaded tomatoes into the hot oil. Fry for 5 minutes or until golden brown. Remove tomatoes from oil with tongs or a wire skimmer and drain on paper towel-lined plates. Serve immediately with Roma Tomato Jam (pg. 82) and Black-Eyed Pea Relish (pg. 80).

Fried Green Tomato BLT

Serves 4

This fun, tasty sandwich uses a couple of southern favorites – fried green tomatoes and pimento cheese. The addition of the aromatic applewood smoked bacon and lightly grilling this sandwich to finish will leave a big impression. You may never go back to a plain old BLT.

3 to 4 firm green tomatoes, cored and sliced into 1/2 inch
  slices (follow recipe for Boathouse Fried Green Tomatoes)
1/2 cup Boathouse Pimento Cheese (pg. 44)
8 slices of brioche bread or firm white (Pullman) bread
6 tablespoons soft butter
1 cup fresh arugula leaves
2 to 3 very ripe tomatoes,
  cored and sliced into 1/2-inch slices
6 to 8 slices cooked applewood smoked bacon

Prepare the fried green tomatoes according to the recipe and keep warm. Spread 4 of the bread slices with pimento cheese, then spread the softened butter on all of the bread slices. Heat a non-stick skillet over medium heat and lay the pimento cheese bread slice, butter side down. Top with some arugula leaves, fried green tomato slice, bacon and top it off with the other buttered bread slice. Cook until golden brown, about 3 to 5 minutes. Flip over and continue cooking for another 3 to 5 minutes until golden brown.

85

Fried Okra with Boathouse Spicy Ranch

Serves 6-8 as a side dish

People from "off" don't eat okra – they just don't know any better. Lightly fried okra is a delicacy to be enjoyed. Introduced by the slaves from West Africa, okra is one of the lingering legacies of African foods that played a major part in shaping southern cuisine. Some mistakenly believe okra to be Cajun food, but okra was brought to Charleston long before it surfaced in New Orleans. The spicy ranch dipping sauce is the perfect finish for fried okra.

3 cups vegetable or peanut oil for frying
2 pounds fresh okra, stems removed and
   cut into 1/4 inch pieces
1 cup buttermilk
2 cups Boathouse Breading Mix (pg. 51)
2 cups spicy ranch dipping sauce

FOR THE BOATHOUSE SPICY RANCH DIPPING SAUCE:
1 shallot, minced
1 teaspoon onion powder
1 teaspoon garlic powder
2 cups mayo
1 cup buttermilk
1/2 cup half and half
1 tablespoon chopped parsley
2 teaspoons chopped dill
1 chipotle chile, minced

To prepare the spicy ranch, place all of the ingredients in a medium bowl and whisk together until smooth.

In a sauce pot, heat the oil to 350 degrees. Place the okra in a bowl and cover with buttermilk. Allow to marinate while the oil heats. Drain okra well. In another bowl, toss okra with the Boathouse Breading Mix until well coated. Fry in batches in the hot oil until golden brown and crisp, about 3 to 5 minutes. Drain on paper towel-lined plates. Serve hot with spicy ranch on the side.

Charleston Okra Soup

Serves 8

Now here's okra the way it was meant to be enjoyed. This important vegetable of African origin has a sticky quality when cut. This "ooze," as some have labeled it, was valued for its thickening properties for soups, gumbos and pilau. Okra soups or gumbos can be found in many historic Charleston recipe books. This is a new twist on an old favorite.

1 beef bone with lots of meat
3 slices applewood smoked bacon
1 onion, chopped
3 tablespoons olive oil
5 garlic cloves, minced fine
8 tomatoes, chopped
3 pounds fresh okra, cut into 1-inch pieces
3 tablespoons brown sugar
Salt and fresh-ground black pepper

Place the beef bone and the bacon in a large pot and cover with 10 cups of water. Simmer for 2 hours. Strain beef bone and bacon, reserving the stock. In another pot, heat the olive oil and sauté the onion and garlic until softened. Add the tomatoes and cook for 5 minutes.

Add reserved stock and bring to a simmer. Add the okra. Simmer soup for 20 minutes. Chop the beef and bacon and add to mixture. Season with brown sugar, salt and fresh-ground black pepper.

86

Boathouse Steam Pot

Serves 6

This dish comes from an early colonial recipe using what was available. The Native Americans showed colonists how to make a broth using pine bark and tree roots purported to have medicinal qualities. The combination of smoky bacon, Tasso ham and fresh marjoram will provide the authentic flavors for this recipe. Fresh fish is always the best choice, and be sure the marjoram is fresh as well.

FOR THE BROTH:
2 tablespoons olive oil
3 slices applewood smoked bacon, chopped
1/4 pound Tasso ham, diced
1 small onion, diced
3 cloves garlic, smashed
2 jalapenos, minced (with seeds)
3 cups fish stock or clam juice (bottled version is okay)
4 cups fresh roma tomatoes, chopped. Reserve 1 cup.
3 cups canned whole tomatoes
1 sprig marjoram (wild oregano)
Salt and fresh-ground black pepper

Heat the olive oil in large pot or deep skillet just until smoking. Add the bacon and Tasso ham, cooking until bacon is slightly crispy. Add the onion and garlic, cooking for 5 to 7 minutes or until onion is brown, stirring occasionally. Add the jalapenos and cook for 1 minute. Add the fish stock/clam juice, 3 cups of the chopped roma tomatoes, canned tomatoes and the marjoram. Simmer the mixture for 15 to 20 minutes, stirring occasionally.

Puree the broth in a blender, food processor or with a handheld emulsion blender until fine. Strain broth or leave it as is. Set aside for use or let it cool and then refrigerate.

FOR THE STEW:
3 tablespoons olive oil
2 dozen littleneck clams (Breach Inlet are the best!)
1 cup white wine
2 dozen large sea scallops with "foot" removed
2 dozen mussels
1 pound shrimp (26/30 count or larger)
2 pounds assorted fish (grouper, mahi-mahi, salmon, tuna, whatever is available)
Reserved broth

To finish the stew, heat the olive oil over medium heat in a heavy-bottomed sauce pan. Add the clams and cover pot to allow clams to steam partially. When clams are just about open (5 minutes), add the white wine and cook until reduced by half. Add the scallops, mussels, shrimp, fish and broth, bringing to a simmer. Cover stew, allowing seafood to cook, about 5 minutes. Add the reserved chopped tomato and serve.

88

Pan Fried Flounder with Corn-Crab Relish

Serves 6

Many youngsters looked forward to the day when they were deemed old enough to go flounder gigging with Dad. Slow trolling at night, aided by a light on the bow of a small boat, patience and concentration were required to spot only the eyes of the flounder reflecting, the body of the fish concealed on the bottom. The reward for the adventurous evening was pan fried flounder, a real treat by anyone's standards. The corn-crab relish is a great addition to the simple fried fish.

5 ears yellow sweet corn
Six 6- to 7-ounce flounder filets
Salt and fresh-ground black pepper
1 cup fine ground cornmeal
1 cup vegetable or canola oil
1 plum tomato, diced
2 tablespoons chopped cilantro
1 lime, juiced
2 jalapenos, seeded, membranes
  removed and minced fine
1 shallot, minced fine
1/2 pound lump crab meat
1 lemon

Preheat oven to 400 degrees. Place the corn on a baking sheet and roast in the husk for 20 minutes. Allow to cool before removing the kernels.

Season the flounder with salt and fresh-ground black pepper. Lightly dredge the flounder filets in the cornmeal. In a large skillet, heat the oil just until smoking. Quickly pan fry flounder for 2 to 3 minutes on each side, remove from pan and drain on paper towel-lined plates.

In a bowl, toss remaining ingredients along with the reserved roasted corn kernels. Serve on top of flounder and squeeze lemon over everything.

89

Pan Roasted Carolina Wahoo with Okra, Tomato, Bacon and Fresh Corn Stew

Serves 4

This versatile fish is widely found in the Atlantic waters of the South. Wahoo is one of the sea's great predators, an exciting fish with a lot of fight on the hook and a delicious meal at the table. This stew, created by the Boathouse chefs, is a perfect to complement the delicious wahoo fillets.

FOR THE FISH:
4 8-ounce fresh wahoo fillets
Salt and fresh-ground black pepper

Season the wahoo fillets with salt and pepper. Heat the oil in a large skillet over medium-high heat. Add wahoo fillets and cook for 3 to 5 minutes or until nicely seared, then turn over and cook for another 3 to 5 minutes. Remove from pan, and keep warm for immediate use

FOR THE STEW:
3 tablespoons vegetable or canola oil
1/2-pound bacon, diced
2 garlic cloves, minced
2 onions, diced fine
4 to 5 ears sweet corn, shucked and kernels cut off
3 large very ripe tomatoes, chopped roughly
1/2 pound fresh okra, sliced
1 cup chicken stock or bottled clam juice
4 tablespoons chopped parsley

In the same pan over medium heat, add the bacon and render until crispy. Add the garlic and onions, cooking for 5 minutes or until onions start to brown. Add the corn and tomatoes, cooking for 5 to10 minutes. Add the okra and stock or clam juice. Cook stew until slightly thick. Serve by portioning the stew into large bowls, then placing wahoo on top. Garnish with chopped fresh flat leaf parsley.

By the time you are a man, there will be at least 20 wagons coming to town.

– Charles Cotesworth Pinckney recalling a conversation with his father in 1753 on seeing a wagon of produce entering Charles Towne.

90

Chipotle Black Coffee Barbecue Ribs
Serves 10

The chipotle, black coffee sauce is a great finish for the baby back ribs seasoned overnight with the dry rub. Try preparing the ribs a day ahead and then grill over an open fire, continuously basting with the sauce.

FOR THE DRY RUB:
1 cup paprika
1 cup chili powder
4 tablespoons cumin
4 tablespoons kosher salt
1/2 cup fresh-ground black pepper
1/2 cup chopped garlic
1 cup Boathouse Cajun seasoning
10 pounds baby back ribs

Prepare the dry rub by mixing all the spices together, including the chopped garlic. Generously rub the spice mixture on to the ribs and allow them to marinate overnight.

FOR THE SAUCE:
1 onion, chopped
4 tablespoons garlic, minced
2 cups red wine vinegar
2 chipotle chilies
6 cups strong black coffee
1 cup molasses
2 cups tamarind pulp
2 cups ketchup
4 cups chicken, beef or pork stock
4 tablespoons dry mustard powder (Coleman's)

Preheat the oven to 300 degrees. Combine the ingredients for the sauce in a large roasting pan. Whisk to incorporate well. Position the marinated ribs into the roasting pan in an upright fashion. Cover the pan with foil and place in oven. Slowly cook the ribs for 3 to 4 hours.

After removing from oven, carefully remove ribs from pan and cool to room temperature. Pour the sauce from roasting pan into a sauce pan and bring to a simmer. Skim fat off the sauce as it slowly cooks. Continue simmering until it reaches a barbeque sauce consistency. Eat the ribs as they are with the sauce, or place them on a hot grill for a more smoky taste and texture.

93

A mountain man likes his coffee strong enough to float an iron wedge and likker strong enough to make a rabbit spit in a bulldog's face.

– Mountain folk-lore

Salmon Cakes with Fresh Dill and Cucumbers

Serves 6

Another type of anadromous fish, salmon has become popular in the 20th century as modern transportation and refrigeration made it available in the Carolinas. The key to this dish is to buy the best, freshest salmon available. The dill and cucumber topping is a nice surprise and dresses up this simple dish.

FOR THE SALMON CAKES:
1/2 gallon water
4 lemons, juiced
1 cup white wine
2 bay leaves
2 celery ribs, chopped
1 large onion, chopped
10 peppercorns
2 thyme sprigs
1 1/2 pounds salmon fillet, skinned and cut into large pieces
2 tablespoons Dijon mustard
1 egg
4 tablespoons mayo
1 small red onion, minced fine
1/2 cup bread crumbs
Salt and fresh-ground black pepper
1/2 cup cornmeal
1/2 cup all purpose flour
4 tablespoons vegetable or canola oil

In a medium sauce pot, bring the first 8 ingredients to a boil (use only juice from 2 of the lemons). Turn down to simmer and cook for 10 minutes. Strain and bring back to a gentle simmer. Add the salmon and poach gently for 15 to 20 minutes. (Do not let the mixture boil.)

Strain the salmon and discard liquid. Lay salmon out on a cooking sheet to cool.

Once cool, crumble the salmon into small pieces in a mixing bowl. Add the Dijon mustard, egg, mayo and red onion and mix well. Add the bread crumbs and gently mix. You still want chunks of salmon, so don't over mix. Combine the cornmeal and flour together in a container. Form the salmon mixture into 6 equal sized patties. Lightly coat with the cornmeal mixture.

FOR THE DILL AND CUCUMBER TOPPING:
1 English cucumber, peeled
2 tablespoons rice wine vinegar
2 tablespoons extra virgin olive oil
2 teaspoons chopped fresh dill
Salt and fresh-ground black pepper

Slice the cucumbers lengthwise on a mandolin or with a knife into thin strips. Combine the cucumbers with the vinegar, olive oil and chopped dill. Season with salt and pepper.

To finish the dish, heat the oil over medium heat in a large skillet. Sauté the cakes on one side until light golden brown, about 3 minutes. Flip cakes over and cook for 3 more minutes. Remove from pan and place on paper towel-lined plate for 1 minute. Place cakes on serving plate and garnish with cucumber mixture on top.

94

Peach Tarte Tatin with Carolina Gold Rice Pudding & Shrewsberry Cookies

Makes 8 servings

Fruit tartes have been enjoyed in the Lowcountry for centuries. This tarte makes use of one of the great delights of the summer season – fresh peaches. The tarte is served with another great heritage food – rice pudding.

FOR THE PEACH TARTE:
4 peaches, halved with pit removed
1 pound granulated sugar
3 ounces butter
2 sheets puff pastry
1/2 cup water

Over medium-high heat combine granulated sugar and water and cook until mixture reaches light brown color. Remove from heat and whisk in the butter. While mixture is still warm, ladle the caramel sauce and cover bottom of 8 muffin tins. Place peach halves, cut side down into the caramel. Cover the peaches with cut circles of the puff pastry. Be sure to cut the circles of puff pastry just slightly larger than the muffin tin circles, as the pastry will shrink while cooking. Bake at 350 degrees for about 18 minutes, remove from oven and turn over onto work surface. Carefully lift each tart onto serving dish.

FOR THE RICE:
3/4 cup Carolina Gold Rice (basmati can be substituted)
1 cup water
1 quart milk

Over medium heat, add rice to the water and start to cook. While the mixture is cooking, add the milk 1 cup at a time until the liquid is absorbed. Process the rice through a food mill, or push through a fine-meshed sieve.

FOR THE CUSTARD:
1 quart heavy cream
12 ounces granulated sugar
13 egg yolks
3 whole eggs
1/2 vanilla bean, scraped of the inside
2 ounces orange zest

Over medium heat, warm the heavy cream and vanilla bean scrapings. Whisk the sugar into warmed cream and cook until granules dissolve. Combine the eggs and egg yolks in a glass mixing bowl. Temper the cream into the eggs a few ounces at a time. Finally, add the orange zest and milled rice and thoroughly mix until smooth. Pour mixture into 8 individual oven safe soufflé baking dishes, 8 to 10 ounces each. Cook in water bath on 350 degrees for 30 to 40 minutes, or until middle barely moves.

CHEF'S NOTE: A water bath is about 1 inch of water in a large roasting pan with soufflé or other baking dishes placed in the water for baking.

FOR THE SHREWSBERRY COOKIES:
3/4 pound granulated sugar
5 ounces butter, melted
4 eggs
1 pound all purpose flour
1 tablespoons nutmeg or mace

Sift sugar and nutmeg or mace into the flour. Add beaten eggs and mix until well incorporated in the flour mixture. Pour in melted butter and mix until dough is relatively stiff. Roll dough thin with rolling pin and cut into 3-inch circles using a dough cutter or tin can. Sprinkle with granulated sugar and bake on 350 degrees for 10 to 12 minutes.

To finish the dessert, place the Carolina Gold Rice pudding in center of a serving dish. Place peach tart next to it and garnish the dish with a few cookies.

95

"Free Form" Peach Pie

Serves 6-8

We love peaches any way we can get them. This peach pie recipe is a real treat and also works with apples or any type of fresh berry for a perfect summertime dessert.

FOR THE PASTRY DOUGH:
2 cups all purpose flour
3 tablespoons sugar
1/4 teaspoon salt
1 lemon, zest only, grated fine
1 orange, zest only, grated fine
3⁄4 cup butter, cold, cut into cubes
1 egg yolk
2 tablespoons ice water

In a medium-sized bowl, combine the flour, sugar, salt and the lemon and orange zest. Add the butter and work it with your fingers until the mixture resembles coarse meal. Add the yolk and water, working quickly to form dough. Work the dough just enough so that it comes together. Do not knead. Allow dough to rest for at least 2 hours in the refrigerator.

FOR THE FILLING:
6 ripe peaches, chopped
2 lemons, juiced
5 tablespoons sugar
2 teaspoons flour
1⁄2 vanilla bean, scraped
1 egg beaten with a few drops of water

Prepare the filling by combining the peaches with the lemon juice, sugar, flour and vanilla bean.

Preheat the oven to 350 degrees. Once the dough has rested, roll the dough into a large circle about 1/2-inch thick. Place the filling in the center leaving about 1 inch around the perimeter of the dough. Working in one direction, fold a portion of dough into the center. Continue folding until all dough is "wrapped" around and there is a small hole in the center, and only a small portion of the filling showing. Brush dough with the beaten egg. Bake the peach pie for 20 to 25 minutes until light golden brown and the filling is bubbly. Serve warm.

97

For a recipe that will truly make the heart merry,
Tis a pound of figs, well-seasoned in sherry;
Then stuff with pecans and raisins sweet,
Roll thin and sugar, they are complete.

– 19th century recipe for stuffed figs

FALL

After the inevitably long, hot summer, fall brings much needed relief from Lowcountry temperatures. Second season crops may still be maturing, but, traditionally, fall is a time of transition, wrapping up the growing season and preparing for winter.

While the "summer people" enjoy the mountains during the heat of the year, everyone and then some return in the fall. The moss-strewn live-oaks of the coast offer their own subtle beauty, but they lack the colorful enticements offered by the hardwoods of the mountains. Visiting the mountains for "leaf change" is as much a tradition as Hoppin' John on New Year's Day or fireworks on the Fourth. The mountain's autumn colors that explode in a riot of red, orange and yellow lure thousands of visitors.

On the coast, the fall season is excellent for fishing, particularly offshore. Inshore, the fishing is great for spot-tail bass, spotted sea-trout and bluefish. Flounder is also plentiful through the fall.

Recreational harvesting of oysters and clams is legal beginning in September. Mid-September signals the beginning of a 60-day shrimp baiting season. The season always opens on a Friday and, by the first night, lighted boats in the harbor appear like a thousand giant fireflies; hopeful

Sweet Potato or Yam?

Most people treat "sweet potato" and "yam" as interchangeable terms for the delectable fall tuber enjoyed in many dishes. They are actually two unrelated root vegetables. The sweet potato (Ipomoea batatas) is native to America. Yams (dioscorea species) are native to West Africa. Sweet potatoes are typically moist, sweet and high in beta carotene, characteristics not enjoyed by the dry and starchy yam.

In the mid-20th century, farmers introduced into the marketplace sweet potatoes with a deeper orange color. These popular sweet potatoes were named "yams" to distinguish them from other varietals, certainly adding confusion to the kitchens of America. Since then, the names have been used interchangeably. In the United States, whether it's called a sweet potato or a yam, you're likely enjoying a sweet potato.

boaters throw their cast nets over carefully placed soft-ball sized spheres of fishmeal and clay designed to attract shrimp on the incoming tide.

Each boat may take up to 48 quarts of the delicious white shrimp per day, the perfect amount to fill a large cooler. Any husband dragging home in the middle of the night, dirty, tired and smelling of shrimp and beer is redeemed to his wife if he arrives with a cooler of shrimp for the freezer. With or without bait, casting for white shrimp in the coastal creeks and rivers in September and October yields tasty rewards.

Hunting is another ritual, and, for some, even a rite of passage. The lengthy deer season perpetuates the pursuit of one of the oldest food sources native to the Carolinas. Hunted by the Native Americans and throughout the history of the Carolinas, whitetail deer are still valued for sport and food. Dove season opens in September; migratory birds may be hunted in November. Many Carolina families maintain a tradition of hunting on Thanksgiving Day, the first day of the small game season for quail, rabbit, raccoon, fox and beaver. Boathouse recipes for Roasted Dove (pg. 120) and Roasted Venison (pg. 127) testify to the enduring tradition and enjoyment of wild game.

Charlestonians visiting the mountains in autumn often return with a car full of the culinary bounty of the highlands: pepper jelly, the vegetable relish known as chow chow, ats jaar pickles, fig preserves.

The North Carolina mountains have become synonymous with the love of apples. The terrain and climate are well suited for apple growing. Still enthusiastically observed, the North Carolina Apple Festival, celebrated each year on Labor Day weekend, was first celebrated in 1938. Mountain residents have long enjoyed getting together to make apple butter. The preferred method is to cook the apples mixed with cider, sorghum, nutmeg and cinnamon in large outdoor cauldrons, a cooking process that lasts well into the night. Cooking apple butter is as much a social tradition as it is a culinary one. Driving through the mountains in September and October, one encounters many an entrepreneur extolling the virtues of his own cider, apples and apple butter from the back of a pickup truck parked alongside the road.

By October, root vegetables are ready for harvest, the most popular being the sweet potato. Carolinians have celebrated this harvest for centuries with an array of soufflés, casseroles, pones, puddings and puffs, all, of course, made with sweet potatoes. Sweet potatoes are another example of a food that best can be enjoyed simply – covered in ashes and roasted in the fireplace (or grill). Once they're done, a little butter and brown sugar are the only accompaniments needed.

U.S. Senate Collection

Like cornmeal and grits, sweet potatoes have no social limitations and are as likely to be served under conditions of poverty as they are to be at the most elegant of meals. In the 18th and 19th centuries, sweet potatoes were stored above ground in potato banks made with dirt and straw.

The sweet potato found its way into South Carolina lore through a painting of Revolutionary War hero General Francis Marion by Charlestonian John Blake White. Marion and a British officer agreed to meet to discuss a prisoner exchange. The British officer was blindfolded and taken to Marion's encampment in the swamps. After business was concluded, Marion invited the guest to stay for dinner. The Brit was shocked to see the evening's fare consisted only of water and sweet potatoes. "But surely, general," said the British officer, "this cannot be your ordinary fare." "Indeed, sir, it is," Marion replied, "and we are fortunate on this occasion, entertaining company, to have more than our usual allowance."

Upon returning to file his report with his superiors, the British officer reported, "I have seen the American general and his officers. They serve without pay and almost without clothes, living on roots and drinking water; and all for Liberty! What chance have we against such men?"

While there are many culinary similarities between Charleston and the mountains, there are also some distinct differences. For example, refined sugar often was hard to get or too expensive no matter where you were in the Carolinas. Sweeteners came from honey or cane syrup in the Lowcountry and sorghum syrup in the mountains. Both were harvested in the fall months, crushed in a mule-powered mill and cooked to

101

In Sarah Rutledge's Carolina Housewife, *published in 1847, there are 300 recipes using either rice or corn.*

the desired consistency. While both cane and sorghum syrup are sweet, the tastes are very different.

Nuts are also affected by geography. The Lowcountry yields pecans; the mountains offer black walnuts, chestnuts and hickory nuts. While planters may have specialized in cotton or rice as a cash crop, every planter also cultivated other crops to serve the needs of his family. A few acres devoted to corn, vegetables and sugar cane usually complemented the fruit and nut trees on the plantation. Roasted pecans make a delightful snack; pecans are also a tasty enhancement to fall meat dishes and desserts alike. Consider the Pecan Crusted Quail with Molasses (pg. 126), which brings together many of the favorite foods of fall. Pecans make marvelous pies and nut cakes, a treat during the holiday season.

Favored for their strong, oily flavor, black walnuts thrive in the mountains. They are rich in protein and minerals and serve as a tasty and valuable snack. Hickory nuts are sweet and flavorful, growing wild in the mountains. Additionally, the hickory tree was favored for its hard wood, used to make the stock or handle for a number of farm tools and gunstocks.

Perhaps the most productive nut tree of the mountains was the native chestnut. Chestnuts were used for breads and dressings, providing a sweet, nutty flavor. The timber from the large chestnut trees was preferred for fence rails and posts. Finally, bees extracted a delicious honey from the chestnut blossoms. It was common for chestnut trees to grow more than 120-feet tall with massive trunks exceeding six feet in diameter. Most unfortunately, the introduction of Chinese and English chestnut trees to America caused a blight in the 1920s. By 1950, the American Chestnut tree was no more. Even today, while seedlings still sprout from the dead trunks of older trees, they die before bearing fruit.

One of the foods most significant to Charlestonians' cultural and economic history was Carolina Gold Rice. In 1685, Dutch ships traveling from Madagascar to New England landed in Charles Towne. Ship's Captain John Thurber presented the colonists a peck of rice in thanks for their assistance. Dr. Henry Woodward, a surgeon and planter, established rice in the swamps along the Ashley and Cooper Rivers. By

Carolina Gold Rice

Charles Towne rice took the name "Carolina Gold," said to be named for the golden color of the outer husk before harvest. The name could have just as easily been earned through the enormous wealth it brought to the growing planter class along the coast. The rice economy, though, came with a cost. The labor-intensive process gave rise to the large imports of human cargo – slaves – to cultivate and harvest these crops. These West African slaves came with the skills and experience needed to grow rice.

After the Civil War and emancipation, planters did not have the available labor to support their large number of acres in cultivation. While rice cultivation continued, the size of the harvest never again approached pre-war levels. Hurricanes in 1880 and 1883 had a detrimental impact on the industry, but the killing blow was the hurricane of 1911, known as the "Duncan Storm," which hit just before harvest. The entire crop was lost, and the rice fields were spoiled by salt water.

1700, rice was thriving in Charles Towne, and planters began exporting their crops to other colonies and Europe.

By 1720, rice was the top export of the Carolina colony. Quickly, Charles Towne rice dominated the Carolina economy, creating one of the wealthiest aristocratic societies in the world. By the mid-19th century, more than 75,000 acres were given over to the cultivation of rice, producing more than 160 million pounds of the prized grain. Carolina rice was delicate, with a distinctive flavor that made it the preferred rice throughout the world.

The harvest for Carolina Gold varied significantly, dependent on the weather from late August to fall. In some years with a warmer spring, planters would attempt two rice crops in one growing season. If the seed was planted early enough and evaded a late frost, the rice could be harvested and a second crop attempted. The most significant gambles, with either one or two crops in any year, was avoiding the late frost in spring, hurricane season throughout the growing season or an early frost in the fall.

Ultimately, with the demise of the plantation economy, not even automation could save the Carolina rice industry. The muddy banks of the Carolina rice fields could not support the weight of the new steam-powered tractors used elsewhere in rice cultivation. Commercial production of rice in South Carolina ended, and Carolina Gold ceased to exist commercially.

Once lost, Carolina Gold now is making a comeback through the efforts of a small group of growers dedicated to heritage crops. In 1986, Dr. Richard Schulze, a Savannah ophthalmologist and avid outdoorsman, began cultivating

Carolina Gold rice on a South Carolina plantation once again after receiving 14 pounds of seed from a USDA seed bank. His determination and perseverance has inspired others to plant Carolina Gold, hoping to return this important heritage crop to South Carolina. Currently, there are at least 150 acres of Carolina Gold in cultivation. The prized rice is, once again, available to the public.

In the 18th and 19th centuries, rice dominated in its importance to the economy and culture of the Lowcountry. Many older cookbooks are filled with recipes, ranging from rice breads and rice pie to rice pudding. One generational favorite is "red rice." Rice pilau and red rice recipes are held as family treasures to be passed from one generation to the next. Boathouse Red Rice (pg. 115) is offered by the Boathouse as a tribute to the Charlestonians who have beguiled their own families with this dish for generations.

Taylor with a Double

Southern Country Punch

Pickled Shrimp

Artichoke Relish

Venison Black-Eyed Pea Chili

North Carolina Smoked Trout with Roasted Apple Port Wine Vinaigrette

Boathouse Clam Pasta

Saffron Broth

Boathouse Smoked Gouda Mac'n'Cheese

Shrimp Pilau

Boathouse Red Rice

Boathouse Shrimp and Grits

Crispy Tortilla-Red Chile Crusted Mountain Trout with Smoked Tomato Grits Tostada and Salsa Cru

FALL RECIPES

Smoked Turkey with Skillet Cornbread-Andouille Sausage Stuffing

Roasted Dove with Sweet Potato "Shepard's Pie," Country Ham & Apple Cider-Maple Glaze

Pan Roasted Wreck Bass with Orange Artichoke Relish and Balsamic Butter

Boathouse Blackened Rare Tuna

Grilled Mahi-Mahi with Boathouse Grits and Tarragon Butter

Pecan Crusted Quail with Molasses Vinaigrette

Roasted Venison with Smashed Root Vegetables and Bourbon Glaze

Chicken Fried-Steak with Vidalia Onion Gravy

Sweet Potato Soufflé with Benne Seed Brittle

Huguenot Torte with Apple Marmalade and Fig Ice Cream

Sweet Potato Pie with Benne Seed Crust

Southern Country Punch
Makes 5 servings

Popular party punch to be sipped at the fall steeplechase.

1 cup Jack Daniel's whiskey
1 cup Triple Sec
1 cup sweet and sour mix
4 cups Sprite

Mix all the ingredients together and serve over ice.

Pickled Shrimp
Serves 10-15

Keep a jar of pickled shrimp in the refrigerator to have on hand when guests drop in. This has been a popular coastal and mountain snack for centuries.

4 pounds medium shrimp, peeled and deveined
2 medium yellow onions, diced
1 teaspoon mustard seeds
4 dried chile peppers, chopped
8 garlic cloves, sliced thin
2 teaspoons coriander seeds
1 star anise fruit
1/4 cup champagne vinegar
1/4 cup extra virgin olive oil
3 lemons, juice and zest
1 orange, juice and zest

Combine all ingredients, except shrimp, and mix thoroughly in glass bowl. Set aside. Boil shrimp in seasoned water for two minutes, or until 75 percent done. Strain shrimp from liquid and place immediately in marinade. Cover shrimp with plastic wrap or airtight lid and immediately refrigerate for 5 to 6 hours. Remove from marinade and serve chilled.

Artichoke Relish
Makes 5 cups

Jerusalem artichokes are indigenous to the Lowcountry, and the cool-weather vegetable has graced Carolina tables for centuries. These irregular-shaped tubers can be difficult to clean, so many relish-aficionados place them in hosiery bags or run them through the washing machine to remove all the sand. Jars of artichoke relish are still traded with no small amount of pride. Try this heritage relish on pork, beef or veal.

2 pounds Jerusalem artichokes, trimmed and quartered, or 2 14-ounce cans, drained
2 quarts water
4 lemons, juiced
1 green bell pepper, chopped
1 red bell pepper, chopped
1 yellow bell pepper, chopped
3 medium onions, chopped
2 cups sugar
2 cups cider vinegar
2 tablespoons mustard seeds
1 tablespoon turmeric
Salt and pepper to taste

Place artichokes in a large pot with the water, lemons, peppers, onions, sugar, vinegar, mustard seeds and turmeric. Bring to a boil and simmer uncovered for 20 minutes, stirring frequently until water is reduced and mixture is mostly dry. Season with salt and pepper.

108

Venison Black-Eyed Pea Chili
Serves 4-6

The cool nights of fall are perfect for serving chili. This recipe celebrates hunting season with the marriage of venison and a great Southern favorite – black-eyed peas!

1 cup black-eyed peas, soaked over night and drained
4 tablespoons olive oil
1 pound venison, from the leg or shoulder, trimmed of excess fat and diced fine
6 garlic cloves, minced
1 onion, chopped fine
1 jalapeno, seeded and minced
2 chipotle chilies, chopped
4 medium tomatoes, chopped
4 tablespoons ancho-chile powder
2 teaspoons cumin
1 quart chicken or beef stock
1 12-ounce bottle dark beer
1 tablespoon chopped cilantro, fresh or dried
Salt and fresh-ground black pepper

Simmer the black-eyed peas in water until tender, about 20 minutes.

In a large heavy bottomed sauce pot, heat the olive oil over medium until almost smoking. Add the venison and brown. Remove from pan and set aside.

In the same pan, with oil, add garlic, onions and jalapenos, sautéing until lightly brown. Add chipotles, tomatoes, ancho-chile powder and cumin and cook for 5 minutes.

Return the venison back to the pan along with the stock and beer. Reduce to low heat and slowly cook the chile for 2 1/2 hours until the venison is very tender. Add the cooked black-eyed peas and fresh cilantro. Season the chili with salt and fresh-ground black pepper.

It is time to eat. Here is supper. Black-eyed peas with ham hock . . . fried okra . . . country cornbread . . . sweet potato pie . . . You talk of supping with the gods. You've just done it, for who but a god could have come up with the divine fest of okra?

– James Dickey, *Jericho*

North Carolina Smoked Trout with Roasted Apple Port Wine Vinaigrette

Serves 6-8 as an appetizer

This is a great mountain recipe honoring both the mountain trout and the apple harvest. Mountain residents often enjoyed filets from small speckled trout for breakfast. The larger speckled and rainbow trout filets were generally reserved for dinner. In this recipe, the Boathouse chefs treat you to a tempting dinner appetizer.

FOR THE TROUT:
4 filets, cleaned and pin bones removed
1/2 pound kosher salt
1/2 pound brown sugar
1/2 tablespoon garlic powder
1/2 tablespoon onion powder
1/2 tablespoon nutmeg
1/2 tablespoon ground sage
1/4 tablespoon ground thyme

Lay the trout flat, skin side down, on sheet pan or cookie sheet. Combine the dry ingredients in a mixing bowl. Coat the trout filets with the dry cure mix and refrigerate overnight.

THE NEXT DAY:
Rinse trout with cold water and pat dry with a paper towel. Let trout stand in the refrigerator unwrapped for 1 hour to dry completely. Using the Boathouse smoking method (pg. 168), cook the trout for 1 hour. Cool in refrigerator until slightly chilled.

FOR THE VINAIGRETTE:
3 medium tart apples,
1 shallot, minced
1 cup apple cider
1 cup rice wine vinegar
2 cups, olive oil
1/2 teaspoon crushed red pepper
1/4 teaspoon dry thyme
1 teaspoon parsley flakes
1/8 cup port wine
Salt and pepper to taste
2 cups mixed greens

Peel and slice the apples and toss with port wine. In a 350-degree oven, roast the shallots and apples until soft, about 12 to15 minutes. Mix together all ingredients except oil and seasonings in a food processor and puree. While blending, slowly add the oil. Finish with seasonings, salt and pepper.

FOR THE DISH:
Place the greens in the center of a large serving tray. Peel the skin from the trout and "crumble" the trout over the mixed greens. Finish with the vinaigrette and garnish with minced chive.

111

Boathouse Clam Pasta
Serves 8

Local legend Toby Van Buren, a long-time oysterman, harvests these clams straight out of the waters right next to the Boathouse at Breach Inlet. Toby farms littlenecks and topnecks, both of which are used in the restaurants.

4 tablespoons olive oil
60 Breach Inlet littleneck clams
6 cloves garlic, smashed
3 shallots, minced fine
1 cup white wine
5 cups saffron broth (recipe follows)
3/4 cup sun dried tomatoes, sliced
1/4 pound butter
3 tablespoons finely chopped assorted herbs,
  such as parsley, basil, chives, tarragon,
  oregano (fresh preferred)
Salt and fresh-ground black pepper
2 pounds cooked linguine
2 cups parmesan cheese

Heat olive oil in a large skillet over medium heat. Add the clams and cover with a lid. Partially steam the clams, about 4 minutes. Add garlic and shallots and sauté for 1 minute. Add white wine and reduce by half. Add the Saffron Broth and continue to steam the clams in lid-covered skillet. Once the clams open, add sundried tomatoes and butter. Swirl butter into the sauce to make it creamy and shiny. Finally, add the herbs and pour the clams over hot linguine and garnish with parmesan cheese.

Saffron Broth
Makes 2 quarts

Use this broth with Boathouse Clam Pasta.

3 ribs celery, chopped
2 large carrots, chopped
1 large onion, chopped
2 bay leaves
10 peppercorns
2 sprigs thyme
2 sprigs parsley
2 cups white wine
3 cloves garlic
2 quarts clam juice (bottled version is okay)
*If you have some shrimp shells or fish bones/carcasses,
  add them as well
1/2 tablespoon saffron threads
Salt and fresh-ground black pepper

113

In a large pot, place all of the ingredients except the saffron and bring to a simmer. Cook the stock for 30 minutes. Remove from the heat and add the saffron. Allow the saffron to steep, about 10 to 15 minutes. Carefully strain the stock through a fine sieve and reserve for later use.

Boathouse Smoked Gouda Mac' n' Cheese
Makes 12-16 servings

Mac' n' Cheese is a Southern standard for the fall. Smoked gouda provides a new twist on this traditional dish.

FOR THE SAUCE:
2 tablespoons extra virgin olive oil
1 teaspoon chopped shallot
1 teaspoon chopped garlic
8 ounces cream cheese
3 cups half and half
1 cup heavy cream
3 1/2 cups shredded smoked gouda cheese
1 1/2 cups grated parmesan
Salt and pepper to taste

Over medium heat, sauté the shallots and garlic in the olive oil. Add half and half, heavy cream and cream cheese. While stirring frequently, continue to cook until the mixture just starts to steam. Whisk in gouda and parmesan cheese, cooking for 5 to10 more minutes until cheese is melted and well incorporated. Season with salt and pepper.

Transfer mixture to food processor and puree until smooth or puree with handheld emulsion blender. Pour pureed mixture over your favorite cooked pasta (elbow macaroni, fusili or penne work great).

CHEF'S TIP:
When pureeing sauce in food processor, do so in small batches to avoid bubbling up and overflow.

Shrimp Pilau
Serves 6

This is the Lowcountry version of a ragout or paella. Carolina Gold Rice, a native crop, is best for this homestyle dish, but basmati rice can be substituted. This dish is classic Charleston!

30 medium shrimp, peeled and deveined
4 cups chicken or clam stock (canned is okay)
3 tablespoons olive oil
2 cups Carolina Gold Rice
3 slices apple wood smoked bacon, diced
1 large onion, 1/4-inch dice
2 celery stalks, 1/4-inch dice
1 red bell pepper, 1/4-inch dice
2 teaspoons chopped garlic, about 2 to 3 cloves
1 bay leaf
2 to 3 sprigs thyme, chopped
5 tomatoes, chopped
2 tablespoons chopped parsley

Peel shrimp, reserving the shrimp shells. In a large skillet, heat olive oil over medium heat. Add shrimp shells and sauté until they become light pink. Add the stock and bring to a simmer for about 10 minutes. Strain the stock and return the liquid to the same pan. Bring the broth to a boil and stir in rice. Cook the rice covered, until tender, about 15 minutes. Remove the rice from heat and allow to steam.

In another large skillet over medium heat, cook the bacon until slightly crispy, about 5 to 7 minutes. Add onion, celery, bell pepper and garlic, then sauté for 5 minutes. Add shrimp, along with the bay leaf and thyme, then cook for 7 to 9 more minutes or until the shrimp are just cooked through.

Discard bay leaf. Gently stir the rice into the shrimp mixture. Remove from heat and fold in the tomatoes and chopped parsley. Serve in a large bowl or dinner plate.

114

Boathouse Red Rice
Serves 6 as a side dish

Lowcountry cooks worth their salt have a recipe for red rice. At the Boathouse, we are proud of our recipe that has garnered rave reviews from our customers. This is another dish that says "Lowcountry."

1/2 tablespoon vegetable or canola oil
1/4 pound applewood smoked bacon, diced
1 large onion, diced
1 each red, green and yellow bell pepper, diced
2 celery stalks, diced
2 jalapenos, seeded and diced
1 poblano chile, seeded and diced
2 bay leaves
3 thyme sprigs
1 cup white long grain rice
2 cups peeled, seeded and chopped tomatoes
  (canned is okay out of season)
2 cups chicken stock
1/2 cup chopped parsley

In a large pot, heat the oil over medium heat and add the bacon. Cook bacon until slightly crispy, about 5 to 7 minutes. Add the onion, bell peppers, celery, jalapenos and poblano chile and continue to cook the vegetables until they are tender, about 3 to 5 minutes. Add the bay leaf, thyme, rice and tomatoes. Stir the mixture so the rice is coated with all ingredients. Add the stock and bring to a slow simmer. Simmer the rice for 20 to 25 minutes, covered with a lid. Once the rice is cooked, remove from heat and leave covered for 10 minutes. Add parsley and serve.

CHEF'S NOTE:
At the restaurant, we make a "base" of the vegetables. This can be refrigerated and used in the ratio of 3 parts base: 2 parts water/stock: 1 part rice.

We used to say, 'Why is a Charlestonian like a Chinaman? Because he eats rice and worships his ancestors.' Now we say, 'What's the difference between a Charlestonian and a Chinaman? A Chinaman lives on rice and worships his ancestors, but a Charlestonian lives on his ancestors and worships rice.'

– Sam Stoney, a beloved raconteur, commenting on the poverty in Charleston in the early 20th century.

115

Boathouse Shrimp and Grits
Serves 8

There is likely no other great Lowcountry dish that has been prepared in so many ways as shrimp and grits, tempting Charleston families for centuries. This recipe is offered as a dinner recipe, but shrimp and grits are found on Charleston tables at breakfast, lunch and dinner. Finishing with Boathouse Green Tabasco Sauce gives this traditional dish a new twist.

4 tablespoons vegetable or canola oil
3 pounds shrimp, 26/30 count or larger
1 pound andouille sausage, sliced
3 cloves garlic, minced fine
1 each small red, yellow, green bell pepper, sliced
  into strips (julienne)
1 large red onion, sliced
1 1/2 cups chopped tomatoes
1 tablespoon Boathouse Blackening Seasoning (pg. 178)
1 cup clam juice, vegetable stock or chicken stock
  (canned is okay)
1 1/2 cups Boathouse Green Tabasco Cream Sauce (pg. 178)
5 green onions, sliced
6 cups cooked Boathouse Grits (pg. 51)

TO FINISH THE DISH:
Heat oil in a large skillet over medium high heat until smoking. Add the shrimp followed by the sausage and garlic, sautéing for 1 minute. Next, add the peppers and onions and sauté for 1 more minute. Add the chopped tomatoes and blackening seasoning. Finally, add the clam juice to thin out the sauce (you may not need to use the entire cup).

Place shrimp mixture over a bed of grits and drizzle with Boathouse Green Tabasco Cream Sauce. Garnish with sliced green onions.

Crispy Tortilla-Red Chile Crusted Mountain Trout with Smoked Tomato Grits Tostada and Salsa Cru
Serves 4

Enjoy this new twist on mountain trout – you may never again have it any other way!

FOR THE GRITS:
4 cups cooked Boathouse Grits (pg. 51)
4 tomatoes, smoked and chopped
2 scallions, sliced thinly
Salt and fresh-ground black pepper

Mix the ingredients together and keep warm.

FOR THE SALSA CRU:
1 small red onion, diced
1 red bell pepper, diced
1 yellow bell pepper, diced
1 green bell pepper, diced
1 jalapeno, minced
2 limes, juiced
1/4 cup chopped cilantro
1/4 cup olive oil
Salt and fresh-ground black pepper

Mix all ingredients together and allow the salsa to sit for at least 2 hours so the ingredients have time to develop.

FOR THE TROUT AND THE TOSTADA:
6 6-inch corn tortillas
1/2 cup cornmeal
1 tablespoon ancho-chile powder
1 egg
1/2 cup buttermilk
Salt and fresh-ground black pepper
4 trout filets, head and tail removed
1/2 cup vegetable or canola oil

116

Bake the tortillas until crisp in a 400-degree oven for about 10 minutes. Reserve four of the tortillas for plating. Place the remaining tortillas, cornmeal and ancho-chile powder in a food processor and puree until finely ground. Remove the mixture and place on a baking sheet.

Season the trout with salt and fresh-ground black pepper and lay out on a baking sheet. Combine egg and buttermilk and lightly brush trout with the mixture. Roll trout in the seasoned tortilla-cornmeal mixture until well-coated. Repeat the process with the remaining trout.

In a large cast iron or heavy bottomed skillet, heat oil over medium-high heat until almost smoking. Place trout, flesh side down, and pan fry until light golden brown. Turn the trout over and repeat. Remove the trout and drain on paper towel-lined plate.

For the plating, place one tortilla in the middle of the plate, spooning some of the smoked tomato grits on top. Lay the trout atop the grits and then spoon some of the salsa cru around and on top of the fish. Garnish with fresh cilantro leaves.

117

To catch the fish you must be the fish. But, if you are also what you eat, you must also surely be the fly. What if you try to eat yourself then you become you all over again. Oh the insanity of becoming a fly fisherman. The peace is in doing and not thinking so much.

- Justin W. Felter

Smoked Turkey with Skillet Corn-bread-Andouille Sausage Stuffing
Serves 8-10

Many mountain residents in years past were sustained on wild turkey, fattened on chestnuts and acorns. Today, the turkey is as much a part of Americana as the Thanksgiving celebration built around it. The skillet cornbread here is a great method for cooking that produces an entirely different taste.

TURKEY PREPARATION:
3 gallons water
2 cups salt
2 cups maple syrup
2 cinnamon sticks
10 peppercorns, crushed
4 to 5 bay leaves
1 fresh turkey, about 16 pounds

Combine all the ingredients together in a bowl. Pour the mixture over the turkey in a container large enough to hold the bird and keep it submerged. Let the turkey rest in the brine for 24 hours.

BOATHOUSE SKILLET CORNBREAD:
3 tablespoons vegetable shortening
1 1/4 cups all purpose flour
1 cup white cornmeal
1 cup yellow cornmeal
1 tablespoon baking powder
1 teaspoon salt
3 eggs
2 tablespoons maple syrup
1 1/2 cups milk
3 tablespoons melted butter

Preheat oven to 350 degrees. With the shortening, grease a cast-iron skillet liberally (use a loaf pan if cast iron is unavailable). Mix all dry ingredients together in a medium-sized bowl. Make a well in the dry goods and add the eggs, milk, butter and maple syrup. Slowly mix the wet with the dry until the batter is creamy with no lumps. Pour the batter into the greased skillet and bake for 25 to 30 minutes, or until a toothpick comes out clean when inserted in the middle. Cool the bread to room temperature before crumbling

FOR THE STUFFING:
3 tablespoons olive oil
1 pound andouille sausage, diced
1 onion, minced
2 cloves garlic, minced
3 ribs celery, minced
1/2 cup bourbon
1 recipe skillet cornbread, crumbled
2-3 cups chicken stock
2 teaspoons fresh sage, chopped
1 tablespoon chopped parsley
1 egg

In a large skillet over medium-high heat, sauté the andouille sausage in olive oil for about 1 minute. Add onions, garlic and celery, then sauté for about 2 to 3 minutes. Remove skillet from heat while adding the bourbon to avoid flare up. Let cook down to almost dry. Remove from heat and place in a bowl. Add the skillet cornbread, chicken stock, sage, parsley and egg. Mix well and refrigerate.

TO COMPLETE THE DISH:
Light your grill for smoking the bird using the technique described on pg. 168 or follow manufacturer's guidelines for a store-bought smoker (charcoal works best for this

118

preparation). Remove the turkey from the brine and pat dry. Stuff the cavity of the turkey with the cornbread stuffing. Once the coals have slowed to the appropriate temperature and the wood chips have been applied, place the turkey directly on the wire grill rack. Close the lid and follow the directions in the smoking technique section (pg. 168). Try to maintain a temperature of 250 degrees inside the grill. Cook time should equate to about 10 to 12 minutes per pound.

When the turkey is dark golden-brown and has cooked for the appropriate time, pull the turkey from the grill and allow to rest for at least 20 minutes before carving. Remove stuffing from cavity and serve with the turkey.

119

Perhaps no bread in the world is quite so good as Southern corn bread and perhaps no bread in the world is quite so bad as the Northern imitation of it.

– Mark Twain

Roasted Dove with Sweet Potato "Shepard's Pie," Country Ham & Apple Cider-Maple Glaze
Serves 6

Celebrating the fall dove hunt, we also draw on inspiration provided by mountain recipes and ingredients.

FOR THE DOVE:
6 dove (or squab), washed and dried, cut to remove
  breasts, legs and wings (reserve legs and wings for
  Shepard's Pie)
Salt and fresh-ground black pepper
12 slices country ham
6 tablespoons olive oil

Season each breast with salt and fresh-ground black pepper and wrap with one slice of country ham. In cast iron or heavy-bottomed skillet, heat the oil over medium high heat until smoking and sear the breasts until golden brown, about 3 to 5 minutes. Turn over and continue cooking for another 3 to 5 minutes. Remove from oil and set aside to rest before serving.

FOR THE SHEPARD'S PIE:
4 tablespoons olive oil
Reserved dove legs and wings
Salt and fresh-ground black pepper
5 to 6 cups chicken stock or water
3 large sweet potatoes, well washed
6 tablespoons butter
2 tablespoons maple syrup
2 Vidalia onions, sliced
2 cups assorted wild mushrooms, such as shiitake,
  cremini, and/or oyster, sliced
1 tablespoon chopped flat leaf parsley
1 tablespoon chopped chives

Preheat oven to 400 degrees. Bake the sweet potatoes until tender or until a knife goes in easily when pierced, about 1 hour.

While sweet potatoes are baking, season the legs and wings with salt and pepper.

In a deep and large skillet or roasting pan, heat oil over high heat until smoking. Sear the legs and wings on all sides until golden brown. Decrease heat to medium and cover the legs and wings with the stock, bringing to a simmer. Slowly cook the legs and wings until the meat falls off the bone, about 1 hour. Remove the legs and wings and set aside to cool, reserving the cooking liquid. After the wings and legs have cooled, pick all the meat and reserve for later.

Cut the cooked sweet potatoes in half, lengthwise, and scoop out the pulp. Place the sweet potato pulp in a bowl and reserve the shells. Mash the sweet potato with two tablespoons of butter and the maple syrup until light and fluffy.

In another skillet, melt 2 tablespoons of the remaining butter until it starts to foam, then sauté the Vidalia onion until lightly brown and tender. Set aside to cool.

In the same pan, melt the remaining 2 tablespoons of butter and sauté the mushrooms until they are a light golden brown. Set aside to cool.

To finish the Shepard's Pie, divide the cooled leg and wing meat into each sweet potato shell. Add a layer of cooked onion and garnish with chopped parsley and chives. Add a layer of cooked mushrooms and repeat with chopped parsley and chives. Finally, add a layer of mashed sweet potato and spread evenly. Keep the Shepard's Pie warm in a low-temperature oven until the rest of the dish is ready to serve.

FOR THE APPLE CIDER-MAPLE GLAZE:
2 tablespoons olive oil
1 onion, chopped
2 celery ribs, chopped
1 carrot, peeled and chopped
1 cup maple syrup
1 1/2 cups apple cider
2 cups of the leg/wing cooking juices
2 teaspoons apple cider vinegar
Salt and fresh-ground black pepper

In a medium skillet, heat the olive oil on medium-high heat and sauté onion, celery and carrot until tender, about 5 minutes. Add the maple syrup and caramelize the vegetables, allowing them to cook to a golden brown. Add apple cider, reserved cooking juices and vinegar.

Continue to cook the glaze on medium heat until it is reduced to about 1 cup and is slightly thickened. Strain this mixture and reserve.

To finish the dish, place warm Shepard's Pie in center of large dinner plate. Lay the dove (or squab) breast across the top. Drizzle glaze atop the breast and Shepard's Pie. Garnish with fresh minced flat leaf parsley.

Whiskey isn't the only thing that's been distilled in these hills. The people are a distillation, too, a boiling down of good Scot-Irish stock, refined by mountain summers and winters, and condensed by hard times.

– Charles Kuralt

121

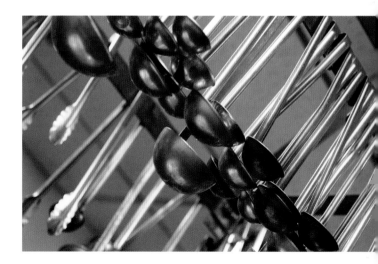

Pan Roasted Wreck Bass with Orange Artichoke Relish and Balsamic Butter
Serves 4

Fall is a great time for catching the plentiful wreck fish. You'll find the orange artichoke relish a great complement.

4 8-ounce wreck bass filets
Salt and fresh-ground black pepper
4 tablespoons olive oil
2 oranges, zest and juice
3/4 cup Artichoke Relish (pg. 108)
1 tablespoon chopped tarragon
1/2 cup balsamic vinegar
1 shallot
1 lemon, juiced
4 tablespoons champagne vinegar
1/2 pound softened butter
3 tablespoons olive oil
1 garlic clove, minced
1 pound spinach

Season the bass with salt and fresh-ground black pepper. In a large skillet over medium-high heat, heat the olive oil until smoking. Add the bass filets, skin side up. Cook the bass filets for 4 to 6 minutes or until slightly crispy and golden brown. Turn over and continue cooking for another 4 to 6 minutes.

While the fish is cooking, heat the artichoke relish and add the orange juice, zest and tarragon. Remove the fish from the pan, set aside and keep warm. In the same pan, sauté the garlic about one minute and then add spinach. Sauté the spinach until it wilts, about 2 minutes.

To make the butter sauce, combine balsamic vinegar, shallots, lemon juice and champagne vinegar in a small sauce pan and slowly simmer over low heat until almost all the liquid has cooked out. Slowly whisk in the butter a teaspoon at a time until all the butter is used and the sauce is shiny and emulsified. Strain the sauce and keep warm.

Place the cooked bass on a plate along with the wilted spinach and top with artichoke relish. Spoon some of the balsamic butter around the fish and serve.

123

Boathouse Blackened Rare Tuna
Serves 6

Yellowfin tuna is a popular fish for "blackened" dishes. The mild flavor and firm texture make it perfect to serve rare and stand up to the blackening seasoning. You'll find the Boathouse Green Tabasco Cream Sauce to be a nice finish for this dish.

2 pounds Yellowfin Tuna, trimmed of sinew
  and bloodline
5 tablespoons Boathouse Blackening Seasoning (pg. 178)
2 tablespoons canola oil
1 cup baby greens
1 cup marinated tomatoes (pg. 78)
1/2 cup Boathouse Green Tabasco Cream Sauce (pg. 177)
Black sesame seeds for garnish

Spread the blackening spice evenly on a large plate. Coat the tuna loin with the spice. Heat a skillet (cast iron works the best) until oil just begins to smoke. Place tuna in the hot oil and quickly sear on all sides. Be sure to sear each side of tuna the same amount of time so that it is evenly seared. Caution: Oil may pop a little upon placing tuna into the pan. Set aside and allow tuna to cool.

Once the tuna has cooled to room temperature, slice the tuna loin with a sharp knife, across the grain, into thin slices. On a serving platter, place mixed greens in the center and arrange the tuna slices atop the greens. Place the marinated tomatoes on top of tuna. Drizzle with Boathouse Green Tabasco Cream Sauce and garnish with sesame seeds.

124

Grilled Mahi-Mahi (Dolphin) with Boathouse Grits and Tarragon Butter
Serves 6

Mahi-mahi is a Hawaiian term that has come into vogue as a reference to dolphin. No – it's not related to the mammals called dolphin frequenting the creeks and rivers inshore. This dolphin can be found offshore and is one of the most beautiful fish in the ocean, with an iridescent bluish green and gold body. You'll love the delicate flavor of this firm, white-meat fish.

FOR THE TARRAGON BUTTER:
4 tablespoons, chopped fresh tarragon
1/2 cup red wine vinegar
1 cup white wine
2 shallots, minced
1/2 pound softened butter

Combine the chopped tarragon with the vinegar, white wine, and shallots, simmering until almost all the liquid has been cooked out. Set aside and allow the mixture to cool. Combine the cooled tarragon mixture with the butter and beat until light and fluffy.

FOR THE GRILLED MAHI-MAHI:
6 6-ounce mahi-mahi filets
Salt and fresh-ground black pepper
Olive oil for brushing the fish
3 cups cooked Boathouse Grits (pg. 51)

Preheat the grill to medium high. Season the mahi-mahi with salt and fresh-ground black pepper. Brush the fish with olive oil and then brush or wipe the grill with olive oil as well. Cook the mahi-mahi, skin side up, on the grill for 3 to 5 minutes. Turn the fish to the other side and continue cooking for another 5 minutes. Remove from grill, and cool for 1 minute.

Serve the fish over the grits and top with the softened tarragon butter.

Pecan Crusted Quail with Molasses Vinaigrette
Serves 4

This time, forget the turkey. This is a great recipe after the morning hunt on Thanksgiving Day, the opening of hunting season. Choose your preference of cane syrup molasses from the Lowcountry or sorghum molasses from the mountains.

4 quail, semi boneless

FOR THE CRUST:
1/2 cup flour
1/2 cup pecans
Salt and fresh-ground black pepper
1 egg
1/2 cup buttermilk
2 cups vegetable or peanut oil for frying

Combine the flour and pecans in a food processor and process until fine. Season quail with salt and fresh-ground black pepper and set aside. Combine the egg with the buttermilk and immerse the quail, one at a time in the mixture. Drain quail and coat with pecan crumbs.

Heat oil to 350 degrees. Fry the quail in the hot oil until golden brown and crispy, about 5 to 7 minutes. Remove from oil and drain on a paper-towel lined plate.

FOR THE VINAIGRETTE:
2 tablespoons sherry vinegar
1 tablespoon Black Strap or sorghum molasses
Salt and fresh-ground black pepper
1/2 cup olive oil
2 bunches watercress or arugula

For the vinaigrette, whisk together the sherry vinegar with the molasses, salt, fresh-ground black pepper and olive oil.

Lay the crispy quail over the arugula and drizzle with the vinaigrette.

126

I realize how much the bond that held us had to do with food.

- Edna Lewis, food writer

Roasted Venison with Smashed Root Vegetables and Bourbon Glaze

Serves 8-10

The hunting season is longer for deer than any other wild game, providing ample opportunity to enjoy venison. Although the early 20th century saw deer populations reach dangerously low levels, strong game management practices have had a significant positive impact. Today, there are more deer in the United States than when the first European colonists arrived in the New World.

In the 18th century, the primary meat for the family meal was venison. Early receipt books provide many ways to prepare and preserve the venison. The meat is rich, flavorful and low in fat, though it has a reputation for being dry and tough. Fast frying or dry roasting can turn this flavorful meat into a dry and tasteless dish. Venison is best when cooked slowly, part of a moist recipe. This preparation will make fans of the most discerning diners.

FOR THE ROASTED VENISON:

2 to 3 pound boneless Venison roast (from the
   leg), cleaned and trimmed (save the trimmings)
Salt and fresh-ground black pepper
2 sprigs rosemary
6 to 8 juniper berries, crushed
1 cup gin (Beefeater)
4 garlic cloves, crushed
1 cup port wine
4 tablespoons olive oil
1 carrot, chopped
2 celery ribs, chopped
1 onion, chopped
2 tablespoons tomato paste
3 cups beef broth or stock
1/2 cup bourbon

Season the venison with salt and pepper. Place in a large dish or plastic storage container and add rosemary, juniper berries, gin, garlic and port wine. Allow the venison to marinate for at least 12 to 24 hours.

FOR THE ROOT VEGETABLES:

2 rutabagas, peeled and diced
2 white turnips, peeled and diced
1 celery root, about 2 pounds, peeled and diced
2 large parsnips, peeled and diced
1 carrot, peeled and diced
5 cups half and half
1 bay leaf
2 garlic cloves

Place rutabagas, turnips, celery root, parsnips, carrot and garlic cloves into salted boiling water, cooking for 15 to 20 minutes or until fork tender. Strain the vegetables from the water and place in a mixing bowl. Add half and half and bay leaf then smash the mixture together with a slotted kitchen spoon or fork.

To finish the dish, preheat the oven to 400 degrees. Remove the venison from the marinade and pat dry with paper towels. Reserve 1/2 cup of the marinade.

In a large cast iron or heavy-bottomed skillet, heat the oil over medium-high heat and sear the venison on all sides until light golden brown. Remove and place in a roasting pan to roast in the oven for 15 to 20 minutes.

While the venison cooks, in the same skillet, sauté any trimmings with the carrots, celery and onion for 5 to 7 minutes. Add the tomato paste and cook for 2 minutes. Add the reserved marinade and beef stock. Allow the mixture to come to a simmer and then add the bourbon. Cook the sauce until slightly thickened, then strain. Keep warm.

Spoon the smashed root vegetables onto an entrée plate or bistro bowl. Slice the venison with a long knife and lay slices over the vegetables. Generously drizzle the bourbon glaze over the venison and root vegetables for best results.

Chicken-Fried Steak with Vidalia Onion Gravy

Serves 6

Chicken-fried steak, sometimes referred to as "country-fried steak," gets its name from the coating, which is browned and crispy, similar to fried chicken. For an inviting flavor, we dredge our steak in buttermilk and flour. Finish with Vidalia onion gravy.

FOR THE VIDALIA ONION GRAVY:

2 tablespoons vegetable or canola oil
2 tablespoons butter
2 medium sized Vidalia onions, sliced thin
1/4 teaspoon chopped fresh thyme
1 garlic clove, minced
3 tablespoons flour
1/2 cup beef broth, chicken as a substitute
2 cups milk
Salt and fresh-ground black pepper

In a skillet over medium heat, melt the butter and oil together. When the butter starts to foam, add the onions and slowly cook, stirring occasionally, until the onions are lightly brown, about 10 to 15 minutes. Add fresh thyme and garlic, then cook for 1 minute. Reduce to low heat and sprinkle in the flour, stirring to avoid lumps. Cook for 5 minutes.

While the flour mixture cooks, heat the beef broth until almost simmering. Once at temperature, add the beef broth to the flour mixture, being sure to stir constantly. When smooth, allow the sauce to cook for 2 to 3 minutes. Slowly add milk and continue cooking for 2 to 3 minutes until lightly thickened. Finish the sauce by seasoning with salt and fresh-ground black pepper.

FOR THE STEAK:

3 cups all purpose flour
1/8 teaspoon cayenne pepper
Salt and fresh-ground black pepper
1/4 teaspoon chopped fresh thyme
6 cube steaks, about 4 to 5 ounces pounded thin
  (about 1/4 inch thick)
1 cup buttermilk
4 to 5 cups peanut oil

In a small bowl combine the flour with the cayenne pepper, salt, fresh-ground black pepper and thyme. In another bowl, combine the cube steaks with the buttermilk and soak for at least 30 minutes.

In a heavy-bottomed sauce pot, heat the peanut oil to 350 degrees. Remove the cube steaks from the buttermilk and shake off excess liquid. Lightly coat the steaks with the seasoned flour. One by one, repeat the process with the remaining steaks. Carefully place the breaded steaks into the hot oil. Be sure to only fry two steaks at a time. Cook the steaks until they are golden brown and crispy, about 3 to 4 minutes per side. Drain the steaks on a paper-towel lined plate. Keep the steaks warm by placing them in a 200-degree oven while the others cook. Serve the steaks with generous amounts of gravy, and garnish with fresh thyme sprigs

CHEF'S NOTE:

Any cut of meat works with this recipe as long as it's pounded thin. Good on pork, chicken and veal.

128

Sweet Potato Soufflé with Benne Seed Brittle

Serves 8

Ahhhhhh . . . the sweet potato. It may be the most versatile of all Southern crops. It can be boiled, grilled, baked or ground; delicious for people and popular in animal feed; can be grown from the sandy, hot soils of the Lowcountry to the cool mountain climes. Here, sweet potatoes are used to create a wonderfully delicate dessert. The addition of the benne seed brittle adds a crispy flourish to the soufflé.

FOR THE SOUFFLÉ:
1/2 cup milk
1/2 cup sugar
1/2 teaspoon salt
3 tablespoons butter
1 teaspoon nutmeg
2 cups sweet potatoes, boiled and mashed
2 eggs, separated
1/2 cup chopped pecans
1 package large marshmallows

Over medium-high heat, scald the milk. In a large mixing bowl, whisk together the potatoes, egg yolks, sugar, salt, butter and nutmeg. Remove the milk from the heat and, while whisking, slowly pour over the potato mixture. Beat the mixture until light and airy. Fold in the pecans. In a separate small mixing bowl, beat the egg whites to stiff peaks and then fold into the potato mixture. Pour entire mixture into greased 8-inch square baking dish (or dish of similar size).

Preheat oven to 350 degrees. Bake potato mixture for 35 to 40 minutes, or until it moves only slightly. Top the soufflé with marshmallows and brown the tops. Remove from oven and let cool before cutting.

FOR THE BENNE SEED BRITTLE:
2 cups sugar
1/2 cup water
4 ounces unsalted butter
1/2 cup corn syrup
1/2 teaspoon vanilla extract
1/2 teaspoon lemon extract
1/2 teaspoon baking soda
1 1/2 tablespoons salt
2 cups toasted benne seed (white sesame seeds can be substituted)

In a large, heavy-bottomed saucepan over medium heat, combine the sugar with the lemon and vanilla extract. Add water, butter and corn syrup, increasing heat to medium high, and bring the mixture to a medium-colored caramel. Remove from heat and quickly whisk in the baking soda and salt. Next, quickly fold in the sesame seeds with a spatula. (Do not try to use the whisk.) Pour mixture onto a non-stick mat or parchment paper sprayed with Pam.

Once the mixture cools (about 3 to 5 minutes), roll out flat with a rolling pin. When completely cooled, break into good-sized pieces.

Cut the soufflé into 8 individual pieces. Place one piece in the center of a serving dish and garnish with pieces of brittle.

131

Huguenot Torte with Apple Marmalade and Fig Ice Cream

Serves 8

The Huguenot Torte, published in *Charleston Receipts*, has now become a standard in the Lowcountry. It was named not for its French origins, but because the recipe's author served this luscious dessert at the Huguenot Tavern, a mid-20th-century hot spot in Charleston. This rendition, served with apple marmalade and fig ice cream, is sure to please.

FOR THE HUGUENOT TORTE:

1 cup chopped toasted pecans
1 medium apple, peeled and diced
2 eggs
1 yolk
3⁄4 cup sugar
1/3 cup flour
Pinch of salt
1 vanilla bean (optional)

132

Whisk together eggs, yolk and sugar until thick and pale. Add the flour, salt and vanilla. Finally, fold in nuts and apples. Bake in an 8 x 8 well-buttered pan at 325 degrees for about 12 to 15 minutes.

FOR THE APPLE MARMALADE:

4 green apples
2 cups sugar
2 lemons, zest and juice reserved
1 tablespoon grated fresh ginger

Peel, core and dice the apples into small pieces. In a small sauce pan, over medium heat, bring sugar, lemon juice and water (enough to cover the sugar) to a boil. When the sugar reaches a medium-colored caramel, add apples, lemon zest and ginger. The mixture will seize at first; then, as the apples release moisture, it will become fluid once again. Continue to cook over low heat until entire mixture is translucent and amber in color. Remove from heat and reserve at room temperature for serving.

FIG ICE CREAM:

1 pint cream
1 pint milk
9 egg yolks
1/2 pound sugar
1 teaspoon vanilla
1 quart figs, rinsed

In a small sauce pan, over medium-high heat, bring cream, milk, half of the sugar and all the figs to a boil. Remove from heat and allow to cool. Blend the mixture in an electric blender or with an handheld emulsion, then return to the heat and bring back to a boil. Whisk together the yolks and remaining sugar in a separate bowl. Slowly add the cream mixture to the egg/sugar mixture, one ladle at a time. Once incorporated, strain the mixture through a fine mesh strainer and cool to room temperature. Refrigerate overnight. Using a store-bought ice cream maker, freeze the mixture according to ice cream maker manufacturer's directions.

TO BUILD THE DESSERT:

Cut the torte into 8 individual pieces. Place 1 piece in the center of a serving plate. Place one scoop of ice cream on top of the torte. Finish the dessert with a small spoonful of apple marmalade. Serve immediately.

Sweet Potato Pie with Benne Seed Crust

Makes one 9-inch pie

This wouldn't be a true Southern cookbook without a sweet potato pie recipe. Sweet potatoes have graced the tables of Carolinians from the mountains to the shore, in good times and bad. This fall season tuber is naturally moist and sweet. Henry VIII believed that a sweet potato pie had aphrodisiacal powers, and he often devoured several pies at a sitting. We can't guarantee this pie will improve your love life, but it will impress your guests!

FOR THE CRUST:
1 cup graham cracker crumbs
2 tablespoons benne seeds
1 tablespoon dark brown sugar
4 tablespoons melted butter

Mix all ingredients together in a medium-sized bowl. Form the mixture into the bottom and sides of a 9-inch pie pan.

FOR THE FILLING:
2 large sweet potatoes
1 1/2 cups heavy cream
3 eggs
1/2 cup dark brown sugar
1/4 cup molasses
1/4 cup maple syrup
1 teaspoon ground cinnamon
1 teaspoon ground allspice
1 teaspoon ground mace
1 teaspoon vanilla extract
Pinch of salt

Preheat the oven to 375 degrees. Place the sweet potatoes on a baking sheet and roast for 1 hour or until soft. Remove potatoes and turn the oven down to 325 degrees.

Allow the sweet potatoes to cool enough so they can be handled. Scoop out the flesh of the potatoes into the bowl of a food processor. Puree the sweet potatoes with heavy cream until smooth. Place the sweet potato mixture into a mixing bowl and whisk in the eggs, sugar, molasses, maple syrup, cinnamon, allspice, mace, vanilla extract and salt. Pour the batter into a prepared pie pan and bake for 30 minutes or until firm. Allow to cool before cutting.

Serve with fresh whipped cream.

133

WINTER

In days of old, mountain winters were, simply put – a season to survive. In the mountains, settlers trusted they had preserved, dried and salted enough food to last through the harsh months ahead. Even in this survivalist mode, mountain people ate well. One mountain resident recalled the winter as "a time for soups and stews, of giant apple cobblers and buttery wedges of corn bread."

By contrast, food in the Lowcountry was plentiful and easily foraged from woods, fields and water. Wild game and shellfish made for lavish spreads at social events, which were commonplace given the mild Charleston winters.

In the 1850s, Emily Wharton Sinkler recorded the traditions of a planter's family.

> This season of Christmas is here. In the first place, staying at Eutaw
> for nearly a week with the house there full of company, involves a good
> deal of brushing up of the children's wardrobes, and then there is to be
> the grandest Christmas Tree ever known which is to be hung with wax
> lights and all manner of gilt things besides presents for the children.

135

The Christmas celebration lasted for a week and each day before breakfast "was the important ceremony of making eggnog in the pantry, in great bowls which were handed around with tall glasses." As part of the ritual, the eggnog was enjoyed in the morning with a slice of cake.

I. Jenkins Mikell, in his 1923 book *Rumbling of the Chariot Wheels*, recalled his favorite traditional social event prior to the Civil War. He noted that the event was set in motion by invitations that read, "We hope to see you and yours at Bleak Hall on the 27th to join us in our Christmas festivities – an oyster roast."

Oysters have been at the center of the cuisine and culture of South Carolina from the early presence of Native Americans, who consumed the mollusks in great quantity. When two English sloops approached the new colony in April 1670, they sailed past a point piled with oyster shells to arrive on the western side of the Ashley River, which they named Albemarle Point. The oyster bank they passed, later named Oyster Point, became the permanent site of the settlement. The Grand Council pronounced in 1679: "We let you know that Oyster Point is the place we do appoint for the port town of which you are to take notice and call it Charles Town." Today, the Oyster Point site is referred to as the "Battery."

136

Native Americans used oysters for food and the shells for tool-making. Archaeology reveals Native American "oyster roasts" more than 4,000 years ago. Among the mysteries left by these early coastal natives are shell rings, enormous rings of organized oyster shells found on the east coast of the United States. First thought to be burial grounds or used for religious ceremonies, research remains inconclusive and the mystery endures. A shell ring at Awendaw, north of Charleston, was equivalent to the size of three football fields.

*He was a bold man
who first swallowed an oyster.*

-Jonathan Swift

Colonists enjoyed this salt water bounty. Often, early land grants made specific mention of the wetlands and oyster banks granted with the highland. In 1845, the state awarded a grant to a gentleman for 400 acres of marshland at Sullivan's Island for an "oyster plantation." In the 19th and 20th centuries, hucksters rolled carts loaded with shucked oysters through the streets of Charleston, servicing eager customers. Raw bars, such as

"Tivoli" on Meeting Street, were common as well. One newspaper ad in 1859 noted, "the rich consumes [sic] oysters with champagne and the poorer classes consume oysters and beer."

Not only were oysters an important food source, the shells had tremendous value. Burning the shells produced lime that was used to stucco buildings and build tabby foundations and fortifications. The oyster shells from a large Native American shell ring on James Island were used to stucco St. Michael's church in the city.

As settlers moved inland and on to the mountains, oysters were symbolic of the Christmas season. While oysters don't play a part in the original Christmas story, they found their place in Carolina traditions surrounding the holiday season. Before modern transportation and refrigeration, December was regarded as the first month cool enough to transport oysters safely inland. Wagons left the coast loaded with oysters packed in seaweed and wet straw to make the trip to eagerly waiting customers.

By the 1850s, ice manufacturing allowed storage and shipping of oysters, fish and shellfish inland, even when the weather was warm. In the 1880s, mechanized ice again improved the ability to ship the prized oysters. By the turn of the 20th century, oysters accounted for almost 50 percent of South Carolina's fishery industry.

Oysters were popular for everyone in the 19th century and were cheaper than beef, chicken or fish. This popularity and demand for oysters provided work for many people on the coast as harvesters and shuckers. Oyster canneries were established across the Carolina coast, employing more than 3,500 people by the 1920s. To hold their workforce, oyster canneries processed okra and tomatoes in the heat of the summer.

North of Charleston at Boone Hall Plantation, the Lowcountry Oyster Festival is held annually in late January. Billed as "The Largest Oyster Roast in the World," the 10,000 celebrants in attendance consume more than 65,000 pounds of oysters and an undetermined amount of cold beer.

The South Carolina Jockey Club
Dinner for Race Week

In addition to the many horse races, Race Week featured a grand dinner on Wednesday evening and the Jockey Club Ball on Friday. Dr. John Irving, of Kensington Plantation, in his 1857 book, *The South Carolina Jockey Club*, writes, "The dinner is always an affair of great enjoyment, got up under the direction of those of the stewards who, from their own love of the good things of this life, know exactly how to provide for the taste of others!"

One such dinner held in 1860 drew rave reviews from all those attending, including the editor of the national racing magazine, *The Spirit of the Times*. Of the spectacular dinner, he offered, "It would seem the entire animal and vegetable kingdom had been placed at the command of the Club's caterer and that heaven itself had furnished the cooks." The menu included a soup course, four varieties of fish, nine kinds of broiled meat or seafood, 10 choices of roasted meat, 14 varieties of game, six vegetables, nine desserts and four "ornaments."

Though our recipes are not written for 10,000, the Boathouse chefs celebrate the enduring oyster heritage of the Lowcountry with three recipes to complement raw or steamed oysters (pg.150).

Winter is a grand time for soups. In the mountains, early settlers were taught by the Cherokee how to prepare dried meat and trout. Beans and other dried vegetables combine nicely with the flavors from a ham bone for cold-season soups.

In Charleston, the most famous soup is she-crab soup, created in the early 20th century. While restaurants today serve she-crab soup year round, it is best in mid-winter when the female crabs are full of roe. The recipe for she-crab soup was first published in *Two Hundred Years of Charleston Cooking* in 1930. It has been a standard dish since. Our Charleston She-Crab Soup (pg. 149) honors this great tradition.

After the lavish cuisine of the Christmas holidays, on New Year's Day, many Charlestonians sit down to a modest meal of Hoppin' John and collard greens – the rice and peas are for good luck and the collards are for plenty of money in the new year. One Lowcountry octogenarian was once asked what happened if a Charlestonian missed Hoppin' John and collards on New Year's Day. He quickly replied, "I have no idea. I don't know anyone who's ever missed a year. Why would you?"

A quintessential Lowcountry dish, Hoppin' John (pg. 154) is a simple combination of rice and peas. The dish dates from "way back." Like many of the great Charleston dishes, Hoppin' John is believed to have originated with the slaves in the 17th century, a preparation carried over from West Africa.

Carolinians, like most Southerners, have a love affair with greens, a group which includes kale, turnip, spinach and mustard greens. At the top of the heap, though, are collard greens.

The preference for greens cooked down in a broth, like many foods, comes from slave traditions. During the era of their bondage, slaves were often given the foods and meat-cuts not wanted by anyone else, cuts like ham hocks and pigs feet. The African-Americans made the most from what they had and cooked greens in a broth flavored by ham hocks.

Oyster Roasts
A great social tradition

The oyster roast is, perhaps, the greatest and most long-lived social tradition in Charleston. Through the fall and winter, Charlestonians gather around a table-sized piece of sheet metal suspended over a wood fire. After a suitable period of time pontificating about the events of the day, accompanied by copious amounts of ice-cold beer, the raw oysters are finally placed on the sheet metal and covered with wet croaker or gunny sacks used to steam them. Just as the prized bivalves pop open, they are shoveled onto tables for the admiring guests armed with gloves and oyster knives.

An oyster roast doesn't need much else beyond cocktail sauce and saltine crackers. Occasionally, a considerate host will also offer hotdogs and chili, a decision usually supported by the oyster roast faithful hoping to distract others; leaving the steamed oysters to the devoted.

Hoppin' John

Sara Rutledge, in her 1847 cookbook, *The Carolina Housewife*, was the first to record the recipe for this famous dish, calling for "one pound of bacon, one pint of red peas, one pint of rice."

The origin of the name Hoppin' John is the subject of much debate. Many 18th- and early 19th-century recipes write the name as Hopping John. One legend suggests that children gathered in the dining room must hop around the table to their seat to be served their peas and rice. Another story is that an old Charleston custom was to invite guests to share a meal by suggesting they "hop in." Still another story tells of a crippled street huckster named Hoppin' John who sold the favorite rice and peas dish from his cart.

Most Charlestonians are not as concerned with the origin of the name as they are about its noteable connection to an annual superstition. Consuming Hoppin' John is thought to bring good luck in the coming year. Rich or poor, black or white – no one would risk their good fortune in the new year by passing up this ritual.

This method of cooking both improves the texture of the greens and eliminates the bitter taste that can be present in the cabbage family. The broth, generally referred to as "pot likker," provides a dip for the cornbread that typically accompanies the dish.

Beyond the promise that collards bring you wealth, folklore also holds that hanging a fresh collard leaf over your door will keep hags and "haints" from crossing through to haunt you. Folklore also suggests that placing a fresh collard leaf on your head will cure a headache. Pot likker is highly recommended for a hangover. Pretty powerful stuff for a leafy green vegetable.

Collards are available through most of the year, but you'll find that the quality and taste of these greens are much better in winter. The Boathouse "Best Ever" Collard Greens (pg. 178) are just that – guaranteed the best collard greens you've ever eaten. The Boathouse chefs add a few other ingredients beyond the ham hock for our "pot likker," and you'll quickly find the demand for these greens well beyond New Year's Day.

Another one of the great social traditions of Charleston has its roots in a minstrel group founded in 1762 to promote concerts and music in the city. Named for St. Cecilia, the patron saint of music, the St. Cecilia Society was responsible for the first symphony orchestra in Charleston. Later, the society sponsored several annual balls and dinners.

The annual St. Cecilia Ball is now held the third Thursday of January and is still the most elegant dinner – some would say stuffy – on the social calendar. One of the last traces of old Charleston society, membership in St. Cecilia passes through the males of the family. The formal dinner and ball is held at Hibernian Hall, located on Meeting Street in Charleston.

The famed "St. Cecilia Punch," offered at the ball, was a delicious concoction of brandy, green tea, rum and champagne. Serving a punch at these elegant outings was the tradition, as opposed to today's style of ordering "a drink" at the bar. Early Charleston recipes offered in *Charleston Receipts* reflect the large number of guests who would be nourished at these balls. The "Charleston Light Dragoon Punch," a deli-

She Crab Soup

Like Hoppin' John, she crab soup (pg. 149) has become synonymous with Charleston cuisine. Many restaurants in the Holy City serve some version of this gastronomic delight. The name 'she crab soup' derives from the use of female crabs in the original recipe.

The dish was created by William Deas, an African-American butler, for the mayor of Charleston. Mayor R. Goodwyn Rhett was to host a dinner for President William H. Taft during a visit to Charleston. Mayor Rhett turned to his butler, an outstanding cook, asking that he prepare something special for this august occasion. Deas served a soup course that quickly became the rage of Charleston – a soup made with she crabs. President Taft was so impressed by the soup that it became a staple at the White House for the remainder of his term.

While she crab soup is served year round now, it's best in mid-winter when the female crabs are full of roe, as originally intended by Deas.

cious recipe including grenadine, curacao and raspberry syrups, rye whiskey, rum, tea leaves, cherries, pineapple, oranges and lemons, provided for 350 servings. Another champagne punch noted in a Charleston lady's receipt book of the 1890s yielded 650 servings, hopefully sufficient to quench the thirsts of even those with a filled dance card.

We offer our recipes for Anytime Party Punch (pg. 148) as a tribute to the centuries-old tradition of the St. Cecilia Ball. Though we've not written it to serve 600 thirsty guests, conversions are available.

One other great social and culinary tradition of Charleston has largely disappeared – Race Week. The first race was held in Charleston on February 1, 1734, on a green adjacent to the Bowling Green House. Through the 1700s, several race tracks were used until the opening of the Washington Race Course in 1792. This one-mile track was located on the property of Hampton Park today.

Unlike the St. Cecilia Society, a membership society, Race Week was an event in which the entire community participated. When the long-anticipated week arrived, businesses closed, court sessions were suspended, schools let out – all made their way to the Washington Race Course. The races were sponsored by the South Carolina Jockey Club, the first jockey club organized in America.

The jockey club had a most interesting rule: "Respectable strangers from abroad, or from other states, are never allowed to pay for admission to any stands on the course. On their arrival, they are immediately considered guests and provided with tickets."

The South Carolina Jockey Club sponsored a club dinner on Wednesday and a grand ball on Friday. Numerous private dinners and parties were held throughout the week. One visitor noted "racing in Charleston maintained an aura of social acceptability that was the envy of other cities." The Jockey Club Ball was the event of the year for Charleston's high society. Meals were lavish and drink plentiful.

Interrupted by the Civil War, race week would never again reach the level that caused the city to cease all other activities. The Jockey Club foundered; its members had

neither the horseflesh nor the resources to bring racing and horse breeding back to its pre-war level. Disbanding in 1900, the South Carolina Jockey Club left its assets to the Charleston Library Society. The gates that once provided entrance to the great Washington Race Course were removed and donated to Belmont Park in Elmont, New York, home to the Belmont Stakes, one leg of the famed Triple Crown.

Though the Charleston races were once four miles on a one-mile track, in 1986, the Charleston Cup reintroduced racing as a steeplechase event. While the Cup is a marvelous social opportunity, the city no longer shuts down for the event, and the lavish balls have not made a comeback. Still, picnics are an important part of the Cup experience.

Winter also brings duck season, generally from mid-December to the end of January. Ducks have been favored since the colonial period. Emily Wharton Sinkler, of Upper St. John's Parish, recorded an interesting recommendation on cooking ducks in her receipt book, circa 1840s:

A raw carrot sliced inside a wild duck and boiled with it will entirely remove the sedgy or fishy taste of the bird. When the duck is half boiled, previous to roasting, take out the carrot, which will have drawn out all the obnoxious taste, and throw it away. Then roast the duck.

An avid golfer in Charleston once remarked that he took up the game only to give himself something to do when it wasn't deer or duck season. Many Carolina families maintain a strong tradition of duck hunting. The old and dormant rice fields along the Ashley and Cooper Rivers are perfect habitats to attract the migrating birds for a snack. The Boathouse chefs offer a recipe for Crispy Duck with Raspberry Port Reduction (pg.161) as a tribute to those cold, wet, but determined, hunters braving the Carolina winter in search of duck for the table.

144

Oysters
Turtle Soup
1 large ham Flat Rock cured
2 ducks
Apples filled with chopped
apple celery & nuts
Café mousse
Small cakes
Olives
Salted almonds
Rolls
Coffee

- The Menu for Harriet Porcher Stoney's "First Dinner" November 12, 1915, honoring her debut.

Red Light

Anytime Party Punch

Cheese Wafers

Charleston She Crab Soup

Boathouse Mignonettes

Boathouse Smoked Salmon

Boathouse Oysters Rockefeller

Spinach-Oyster Salad with Country Ham-Port Wine Dressing and Blue Cheese

Hoppin' John

Country Captain

Roasted Lamb Rack with Benne Seeds and Mint-Lavender Honey Jelly

WINTER RECIPES

Grilled 21-Day Aged NY Strip Steak with Three Sauces

Smoked Garlic-Parsley Butter

Oven Roasted Crispy Duck with Raspberry Port Reduction and Chive Mashed Potatoes

Pan Seared Grouper in Ham Hock Broth over Carolina Gold Rice Cake

Boathouse Butter Poached Lobster Tails with Fresh Lemon

Boathouse Benne Seed Wafers

Boathouse Chocolate Mousse

Buttermilk Ginger Cake with Candied Kumquats, Spiced Crème Fraiche & Caramel Sauce

Chocolate-Praline Charlotte with Butterscotch Sauce

Anytime Party Punch
Yields 3 quarts

When entertaining during the holidays, save yourself time and trouble by making this fabulous punch ahead. Party punches have been part of the Lowcountry social scene for centuries.

15 ounces Southern Comfort
60 ounces Coca Cola
12 ounces soda water
10 ounces cherry juice
5 oranges, juiced
3 lemons, juiced
2 limes, juiced
12 cherries

Mix all ingredients together and pour over ice. Garnish with cherries.

148

Cheese Wafers
Yields 2 dozen wafers

Cheese wafers or cheese straws have been in the Charleston culinary vernacular for many generations. This simple recipe will provoke many compliments. For a new twist, we've added pecans.

1/2 cup butter
1 1/2 cups all purpose flour
1 teaspoon salt
1/2 pound cheddar cheese
1 pinch hot pepper flakes
1 dash hot pepper sauce
3/4 cup pecans (chopped or pieces)

In a stainless steel or glass bowl, cut the butter into the flour with a fork or by hand until mixture resembles coarse meal. Add the salt, cheddar cheese, hot pepper flakes, hot pepper sauce and pecans and mix thoroughly until well incorporated. Roll the mixture into a 2-inch log, wrap with plastic and refrigerate overnight.

Preheat oven to 350 degrees. Remove plastic wrap and cut the dough into discs or "wafers" about 1/4-inch thick. Lay the wafers on a greased baking sheet and bake until golden brown and crisp, about 15 minutes.

Charleston She Crab Soup
Serves 8

This great soup just says CHARLESTON to most people. A menu for she crab was first published in *Two Hundred Years of Charleston Cooking* in 1930. Insist on finding female crabs full of roe to sample the soup the way it was intended. DO NOT take a shortcut -- always start with whole crabs, otherwise you lose most of the great flavor in the soup stock.

1 onion, chopped
3 celery ribs, chopped
2 bay leaves
5 cups water or stock (chicken or vegetable)
6 to 8 female crabs
2 tablespoons butter
1/2 teaspoon mace
1/2 teaspoon allspice
1/2 teaspoon cayenne pepper
3 tablespoons flour
1 cup milk
1 1/2 cups heavy cream
2 tablespoons grated lemon zest
2 tablespoons chopped parsley
Salt and fresh-ground black pepper

Sauté the onion and celery until tender. Add bay leaves, water or stock, and the whole crabs, then cook for 10 minutes. Remove the crabs to cool. Pick out the meat and scrape out the roe, then set aside for later use. Reserve the shells and the cooking liquid. Return the cooking liquid to the pot and bring to a simmer.

Melt the butter in another sauce pot and add the crab shells with the mace, allspice and cayenne. Sauté the crab shells and spices for 2 to 3 minutes. Add the flour to the sautéed mixture and continue cooking for 2 to 3 minutes.

Add the reserved stock and bring to simmer. Reduce heat to low, and cook for 10 minutes. Add the milk and heavy cream, then increase heat to medium-high and bring the soup to a simmer. Strain the soup and add the reserved crab meat and roe. Season with salt and fresh-ground pepper, finishing the soup by adding lemon zest and fresh parsley.

CHEF'S NOTE:
Use the crab shells to make a stock. To make the soup a bit lighter, use less flour.

149

Never have we sampled food that tasted better. When anyone asks us now where do we eat best in the United States, instead of our usual chat of New Orleans, San Francisco, New York City; hereafter Charleston leads the list.

- *New York Herald* food editor Clementine Paddleford after sampling dishes from *Charleston Receipts* in 1951.

Boathouse Mignonettes
Makes 1 cup of each (enough for at least 12 oysters)

We offer three mignonettes to complement your raw or steamed oysters. Choose one that suits the occasion or make all three and let your guests sample and compare.

JALAPENO-LIME MIGNONETTE:
2 to 3 large jalapenos, seeded and diced fine
3 shallots, minced fine
2 tablespoons chopped cilantro
3 limes, juiced
1/2 cup rice wine vinegar
Salt to taste
1/2 tablespoon olive oil

KEY LIME MIGNONETTE:
3/4 cup fresh key lime juice (or Nellie and Joe's)
3 tablespoons honey
2 shallots, minced fine

RED WINE MIGNONETTE:
3/4 cup red wine vinegar
1/4 cup red wine
2 shallots, minced fine
1 teaspoon fresh-ground black pepper
Salt to taste
Sugar to taste

FOR THE MIGNONETTES:
Combine all ingredients and allow to rest for at least 30 minutes to infuse all of the flavors before use.

Boathouse Smoked Salmon
Serves 8-10 as an appetizer

This smoked salmon serves as an excellent starter to any meal or as an hors d'oeuvres with cocktails.

1 3-pound skin-on side of salmon trimmed of excess waste with pin bones removed
1/2 cup kosher salt
1/2 cup brown sugar
1 teaspoon dried thyme
1 teaspoon ground nutmeg
1/2 teaspoon garlic powder
1/2 teaspoon dried sage

Trim the tail of the salmon so that the filet becomes a uniform rectangle. Lay salmon on a cookie sheet with raised edges. Mix the dry ingredients together and coat salmon with the mixture. Put salmon in the refrigerator and allow it to cure for at least 24 hours.

Once cured, carefully rinse off the salt-sugar curing mix. Pat salmon dry and transfer to a wire rack. Set up smoker according to manufacturer's directions (pg. 168). The salmon should smoke for at least 30 minutes. Allow to continue to slow cook on the grill for 1 hour or until desired doneness. Allow to cool thoroughly before slicing.

150

Boathouse Oysters Rockefeller

Serves 6-8

This great dish, created in 1899 at Antoine's Restaurant in New Orleans, quickly made its way to Charleston, evidence alone that Charlestonians can recognize when someone else brings honor to an oyster. The original recipe, created by Jules Alciatore, was said to be so rich that it was named for the richest man in America, John D. Rockefeller. Though often imitated, the original recipe has never been divulged by the famous restaurant. We've put our own touch to Antoine's treatment and proudly offer the Boathouse Oysters Rockefeller.

2 tablespoons olive oil
2 pounds country ham, diced
2 tablespoons garlic, minced
1/2 cup white wine
2 pounds of spinach, trimmed and cleaned
2 cups chilled Boathouse Green Tabasco Cream Sauce
    (pg. 177)
1/2 cup Italian flat leaf parsley, chopped fine
2 tablespoons (about 1 bunch) fresh tarragon,
    chopped fine
1 cup parmesan
Salt and fresh-ground black pepper
30 oysters such as Carolina Cups, Apalachicola's,
    Malpeques or Blue Points, shucked and left in
    half of the shell, then covered with moist towels
    and refrigerated

In a large skillet, heat the oil until it starts to smoke. Add the country ham and cook just until crisp, about 3 to 5 minutes. Add the minced garlic and cook for a minute, stirring so that the garlic doesn't burn. Add the white wine, scraping up the bits that have stuck to the bottom of the pan. Cook the mixture for 2 to 3 more minutes, or until the wine has reduced by half. Remove pan from heat

and add the spinach. Stir spinach until it wilts and is well incorporated with the country ham-garlic mixture. Transfer spinach to a strainer and allow moisture to drain. Place in a medium-sized bowl and refrigerate for 30 minutes.

Preheat broiler in oven to 500 degrees or highest setting, and position one of the racks on the top shelf. Mix the chilled Boathouse Green Tabasco Cream Sauce, chopped parsley, tarragon and parmesan cheese with the spinach. Season this Rockefeller mix with salt and fresh-ground black pepper.

Retrieve the oysters. Spoon approximately 1 tablespoon of mixture on top of each oyster and place on a baking sheet. Place the baking sheet under the broiler and cook the oysters about 1 to 2 minutes or until the tops are golden brown and bubbly. Serve on rock salt with fresh lemon segments.

Oysters are the most tender and delicate of all seafoods. They stay in bed all day and night. They never work or take exercise, are stupendous drinkers, and wait for their meals to come to them.

- Hector Bolitho, *The Glorious Oyster*

152

Spinach-Oyster Salad with Country Ham-Port Wine Dressing and Blue Cheese

Serves 6

Any oyster would be proud to play a role in this enticing salad. The succulent fried oysters atop the spinach and blue cheese, accented with the country ham-port wine dressing, make a great lunch or light dinner.

FOR THE DRESSING:
2 tablespoons olive oil
1/2 pound country ham, diced
1 medium-sized shallot, minced
2 cloves garlic, minced
1/2 cup port wine
3 tablespoons red wine vinegar
2 teaspoons Dijon mustard
3/4 cup olive oil

Heat 2 tablespoons of oil in a large skillet over medium high heat until smoking. Add the diced country ham and cook until the ham just begins to crisp, about 3 to 5 minutes. Add the shallots and garlic and cook for about a minute. Remove skillet from heat and pour in the port wine while scraping the bottom of the pan. Scrape port wine mixture into a bowl and cool to room temperature. Add the vinegar and mustard, then whisk to combine. While whisking, slowly add the olive oil in a steady stream until the dressing is well blended and slightly thick. Set aside for later use.

FOR THE SALAD:
5 cups baby spinach
1 red onion, thinly sliced
2 dozen cherry or grape tomatoes, halved
1 large carrot, shredded
1 cup crumbled blue cheese

For the salad, place the spinach on a large serving platter. Arrange the red onion, tomatoes and carrot on top and sprinkle with the blue cheese.

FOR THE OYSTERS:
3 cups peanut oil
30 oysters, shucked or by the quart,
    packed in their own juice
2 cups cornmeal
Salt and fresh-ground black pepper
2 cups buttermilk

Heat the peanut oil in large, heavy-bottomed saucepan to 350 degrees. Drain the oysters of their natural juice in a colander. Combine the cornmeal with salt and fresh-ground pepper in a shallow bowl. Place the buttermilk in another shallow bowl. Add the oysters to the buttermilk. One by one, transfer the oysters from the buttermilk to the cornmeal, coating them thoroughly with the cornmeal mixture. Once coated, place the oysters on a baking sheet. Carefully drop the oysters into the hot oil, one by one, in batches of 5 or 6 at a time. Cook for 2 to 3 minutes, being sure to turn the oysters once or twice. Remove from oil and drain on paper towels.

Arrange them around the spinach salad and serve immediately. Allow your guests to pour on as much dressing as they desire!

153

Hoppin' John
Serves 8

Thought to bring good luck in the upcoming year, every Charlestonian worth his family name sits down to a meal of Hoppin' John and collards on New Year's Day. This is a simple dish, but the combination of rice and peas, flavored by the ham, has earned generations of devoted fans.

1 cup fresh peas such as black-eyed, pinkeye or crowder
8 cups water
1 small onion, diced
1 carrot, peeled and diced
1 celery stalk, diced
2 smoked ham hocks or about 1/2 pound slab bacon
2 jalapenos, seeds removed and minced
1 bay leaf
2 to 3 thyme sprigs
2 cups basmati rice
1 cup chopped scallions
1/2 cup chopped parsley
1 lemon, juiced

Place the peas in water and bring to a simmer. Add the onion, carrot, celery, ham hock, jalapenos, bay leaf and thyme, continuing to simmer for 20 to 25 minutes until the peas are tender. Drain and reserve the cooking liquid, about 3 1/4 cups, in a sauce pot to cook the rice. Discard vegetables.

Bring cooking liquid to a boil and add the rice. Cover rice with a lid and cook at a simmer for 15 minutes. Remove from heat and allow to finish cooking by steaming, about 10 minutes.

Combine the cooked peas with the cooked rice. Gently fold in the scallions, parsley and lemon juice. Season with salt and fresh-ground black pepper and serve.

Now hopping-john was F. Jasmine's very favorite food. She had always warned them to wave a plate of rice and peas before her nose when she was in her coffin, to make certain there was no mistake; for if a breath of life was left in her, she would sit up and eat, but if she smelled the hopping-john, and did not stir, then they could just nail down the coffin and be certain she was truly dead.

- Carson McCullers, *The Member of the Wedding*

154

Country Captain

Serves 6

A popular dish since the early 19th century, Country Captain has been claimed by many Southern port cities. One story tells the tale of a sea captain, returning with spices from India in the 1800s, who introduced the recipe to the South. Other stories suggest this dish was served by the captain of Indian troops to British soldiers in the 1800s. Either way, Country Captain was served in Charleston and recorded in family recipe books. We've updated the ingredients and offered practical cooking techniques to recreate this dish.

8 bone-in chicken thighs
Salt and fresh-ground black pepper
2 teaspoons vegetable or canola oil
2 large onions, chopped
1 green bell pepper, chopped
2 garlic cloves, minced
1 1/2 tablespoons sweet paprika
1 tablespoon Madras-style curry powder
1/4 teaspoon cayenne pepper
3 tablespoons flour
1 1/2 cups chicken stock
3 tomatoes, chopped
1 bay leaf
1/2 teaspoon fresh thyme, minced
1/2 cup raisins
1 ripe mango, peeled, pitted and diced
1/4 cup chopped cilantro

Season chicken thighs with salt and pepper. In a large pot or Dutch oven, heat oil over medium-high heat until smoking. Brown chicken thighs on the skin side until golden brown. Turn over and repeat browning process. Remove chicken from pot and discard half the residual oil.

Over medium heat, add the onions, bell pepper and garlic, then sauté until tender, about 3 minutes. Add the paprika, curry powder, cayenne pepper and flour. Cook for 3 to 5 minutes, scraping the bits from the bottom of the pan.

Add the stock, tomatoes and bay leaf. Put chicken back into pan and increase heat to bring liquid to a boil. Once it begins to boil, reduce to a simmer until chicken is very tender and almost falling off the bone, about 30 to 35 minutes.

During the last 10 to 15 minutes of cooking, add the thyme, raisins and mango. Garnish with cilantro.

155

Roasted Lamb Rack with Benne Seeds and Mint-Lavender Honey "Jelly"
Serves 6

Lamb gained popularity in the South in the 20th century. The Scot-Irish came to the Carolinas with a taste for mutton, meat of mature sheep. While mutton is still preferred in many countries today, Americans prefer lamb. The Boathouse chefs have given this dish a distinctive Lowcountry flavor with benne seeds and mint-lavender honey jelly.

FOR THE JELLY:
2 jalapenos, chopped
2 tablespoons fresh mint, chopped
3/4 cup rice wine vinegar
1 cup sugar
1 1/2 cups lavender honey
4 tablespoons water
1/2 packet (1 ounce) powdered fruit pectin

Combine the jalapenos, mint, vinegar and sugar in a food processor and puree until fine. Add to a sauce pan, along with the honey, water and pectin. Bring to a boil and simmer for 3 minutes. Strain and set aside to cool.

FOR THE LAMB RACKS:
2 lamb racks, trimmed and frenched
 (a butcher can do that for you)
Salt and fresh-ground black pepper
3 tablespoons vegetable or canola oil
3 tablespoons benne seeds

Preheat oven to 400 degrees. Season lamb racks with salt and pepper. In a large skillet, heat oil over medium-high heat until smoking and sear the racks until golden brown. Turn over and repeat the process. Remove from skillet and allow to rest for 2 minutes.

Place seared lamb racks on a baking sheet and brush with 2 or 3 tablespoons of jelly. Sprinkle lamb with the benne seeds and place in oven to roast for 15 minutes (for medium rare). Remove from oven and allow meat to rest for 10 minutes before carving. Serve with the chilled jelly on the side.

157

The only reason for being a bee that I know of is making honey ... and the only reason for making honey is so I can eat it.

- Winnie the Pooh

Grilled 21-Day Aged NY Strip Steak with Three Sauces

Serves 6

There's nothing like a great steak. Brush with garlic-parsley butter and serve with the Boathouse Worcestershire Sauce and the Boathouse Charred Tomato Vinaigrette for a distinctive, delicious flavor.

6 14-ounce aged NY strip steaks
  (ask butcher to trim excess fat)
Salt and fresh-ground black pepper
4 tablespoons olive oil
3 to 4 thyme branches
1/2 cup Smoked Garlic-Parsley Butter, softened
1 cup Boathouse Worcestershire Sauce (pg. 177)
1 cup Boathouse Charred Tomato Vinaigrette (pg. 54)
1 cup Boathouse Steak Sauce (pg. 177)

Preheat a grill, broiler or skillet until blazing hot. Remove steaks from refrigerator and allow them to come to room temperature. Season steaks well with salt and fresh-ground black pepper, rubbing the seasonings into the meat. Coat the steaks with olive oil and place on grill. Cook 5 to 7 minutes on each side for medium rare.

While the steaks cook, dip a thyme branch into the smoked garlic-parsley butter. Lightly brush steaks with thyme. Make sure butter does not flare up on the grill.

Allow steaks to rest for at least 7 to 10 minutes before carving or serving. Serve with Boathouse Worcestershire Sauce and Boathouse Charred Tomato Vinaigrette.

Smoked Garlic-Parsley Butter

Makes 3 cups

This butter can be made ahead and frozen for future use.

1/2 cup peeled garlic cloves
2 lemons, juiced
4 tablespoons white wine
1/4 cup chopped parsley
1 pound softened butter
Salt and fresh-ground black pepper

In a small pot, bring water to a boil and cook garlic cloves for 3 to 5 minutes or until soft. Drain well and cool. Smoke garlic cloves (see techniques pg. 168) on a wire rack under low heat or indirect heat for about 10 minutes. Puree the smoked garlic with the white wine until it becomes a smooth paste. Scrape smoked garlic into a bowl or stand mixer then add remaining ingredients. Whisk the mixture until light and fluffy. Season with salt and fresh-ground black pepper.

Roll butter into logs using butcher paper or plastic wrap and refrigerate. Slice when needed. The butter freezes well if properly wrapped and sealed.

The only time to eat diet food is while you are waiting for the steak to cook.

- Julia Child

158

Oven Roasted Crispy Duck with Raspberry Port Reduction and Chive Mashed Potatoes

Serves 6

Waterfowl of all types have long been enjoyed in the Carolinas. Many home chefs are not as confident preparing duck as other waterfowl or game. Trying this crispy duck recipe will forever alter your outlook. The raspberry port reduction is an enticing accent to this dish.

FOR THE DUCK:
3 medium skin-on ducks, trimmed of all excess fat
1/2 cup extra virgin olive oil
Salt and pepper

Preheat oven to 300 degrees. Place ducks in a large bowl and cover with oil. Season with salt and pepper, coating ducks thoroughly. Place ducks, breast side up on an oven safe grate in a large roasting pan to allow the excess fat to drip away from the ducks during the roasting process. Roast for 2 1/2 to 3 hours and remove from oven. Increase temperature to 475 degrees, and roast ducks for 12 more minutes, or until the skin is crispy and golden brown. Remove from oven and reserve for later use.

FOR THE RASPBERRY PORT REDUCTION:
32 ounces beef stock (store bought is acceptable)
24 ounces chicken stock
1 cup orange juice
1 cup port (reduced to 1/2 cup over medium heat)
2 pints fresh raspberries
1 cup sugar
2 ounces whole butter, cut into cubes
Salt and pepper

Over medium-low heat, cook the berries and the sugar until well incorporated, and the berries are extremely soft, about 30 minutes. Reserve for later use.

In a medium sauce pan over medium-high heat, reduce beef stock by half. Add chicken stock and reduce again by half. Add the orange juice, port wine and raspberries, then continue to cook over medium-low heat until mixture begins to thicken slightly. Whisk in whole butter. Finish with salt and pepper.

FOR THE CHIVE MASHED POTATOES:
3 pounds Yukon gold potatoes (skin-on, boiled or steamed until fork tender)
4 ounces butter
1 cup whole milk
1/2 cup half and half
1/2 bunch chives, minced
Salt and pepper to taste

Combine cooked potatoes, butter, milk, and half and half in a large bowl, then smash together with a potato masher or heavy-duty whisk. Season with salt, pepper and chives. Mix thoroughly.

FOR THE DISH:
Split the ducks and remove the breast, thigh and leg. Place spoonful of mashed potatoes in center of dinner plate. Arrange breast, leg and thigh around the potatoes and finish by drizzling the raspberry-port reduction over the duck and potatoes. Garnish with fresh minced chive.

161

Pan Seared Grouper in Ham Hock Broth over Carolina Gold Rice Cake

Serves 4

Even in the winter, grouper is plentiful among South Carolina's artificial reefs. Grouper is a popular fish in the South partially because of its availability but also due to the firm, sweet meat of the fish. Most diners enjoy the moist flakey qualities of the fish when prepared. You might notice that grouper finishes with a hint of shrimp. Like many Charlestonians, grouper prefer a diet of shellfish.

FOR THE RICE CAKE:
3/4 cup Carolina Gold Rice
1 1/2 cups water
1 egg
1/2 cup mayonnaise
1/4 cup minced chive and flat leaf parsley
1 cup Japanese bread crumbs (Panko)

162

In a small sauce pan over medium heat, combine the rice with the water and cook, stirring frequently until the water is dissolved. Remove from heat and spread onto a large plate to cool. Once rice has cooled to room temperature, combine cooked rice and egg in mixing bowl. Add mayonnaise and continue folding until thoroughly mixed. Add fresh herbs and 1/4 cup of bread crumbs, mixing until well incorporated. Portion the rice mixture into four evenly sized cakes. Roll the cakes in the remaining bread crumbs and reserve for later use.

FOR THE BROTH:
1 teaspoon olive oil
1 yellow onion, diced
1 carrot, diced
1 celery stalk, diced
1 leek
1 bay leaf
3 sprigs fresh thyme, leaves picked
1 bunch flat leaf parsley, leaves picked and chopped
1/4 cup Marsala wine
1 cup red wine
2 smoked ham hocks
2 cups chicken stock or broth
1 tablespoon butter
Salt and pepper to taste
Juice of one lemon

Heat olive oil in medium-sized sauce pan over medium heat. Add onion, carrot and celery, then cook until onion develops a little color. Deglaze vegetables by adding the red wine and the Marsala wine and continue cooking until the wine has reduced by half. Add leeks, ham hocks, thyme, parsley and chicken stock, then simmer mixture for 1 to 1 1/2 hours. Remove ham hocks and reserve for later use. Strain remaining mixture into a bowl. Finish broth by whisking in whole butter, lemon juice and salt and pepper to taste. Clean the reserved ham hocks and add the meat to the broth

FOR THE DISH:
4 ounces olive oil
4 6-ounce portions fresh grouper
20 cippolini onions
1 leek, halved and sliced
2 roma tomatoes, 1/2 inch diced

In a medium-sized skillet over medium heat with 2 ounces of olive oil, sear the rice cakes until nicely browned on both sides. While rice cakes are cooking, sear grouper in a heavy-bottomed pan with the remaining olive oil over medium-high heat, starting flesh side down, until fish is nicely colored and develops a crispy crust. Turn over, and continue to sear for 2 to 3 more minutes, then remove and finish in 350-degree oven for 2 to 3 minutes. In the same pan, add 1 tablespoon olive oil, cippolini onions, leeks and sauté for 2 minutes. Add broth and cook for 2 more minutes. Finish sauce with fresh tomatoes.

Place Carolina Gold Rice Cakes in center of large pasta bowl or plate with raised rim. Place grouper atop the rice cake, then distribute evenly the vegetable mixture and broth among the four plates. Garnish with whole chive shoots.

Boathouse Butter Poached Lobster Tails with Fresh Lemons
Serves 4

Lobster tails are not typical heritage Lowcountry fare. By the late 20th century, however, their inclusion on any fine menu was both expected and appreciated. There is a steady recreational pursuit of deep-sea lobsters off the South Carolina coast. Whether a Maine lobster or one caught off our own coast, a butter-poached crustacean is a delight.

8 2- to 3-ounce cold water lobster tails
1 1/2 pounds butter, cut into cubes
2 tablespoons water
3 lemons, cut in half

Preheat broiler to 350 degrees. Cut each tail in half right through the shell. Remove vein and release meat from shell, but don't pull all the way out. Lay lobsters, flesh side up, on a baking sheet. Place lobsters in broiler and cook for 3 minutes.

While the lobster cooks, heat water in a small pot until it starts to steam. Whisk in the butter a couple of cubes at a time until the mixture is well blended. Keep warm over low heat. If it gets too hot the mixture will break.

After 3 minutes the lobster should still be opaque, but not cooked through. Place lobster into butter bath and cook for 4 minutes or until the lobsters are cooked. Remove from butter bath and serve with the lemon. Use remaining butter for dipping the poached lobster.

CHEF'S NOTE:
The butter procedure for this recipe is referred to as *beurre monte*. It can also be used to reheat cooked vegetables and for reheating the product with the same method used to make it.

163

Boathouse Benne Seed Wafers
Makes 16-20 wafers

Benne seeds were introduced to Charleston by West African slaves. Commonly called sesame seeds, benne is the Nigerian name that has persisted in Charleston. Africans believed the benne seeds brought good luck, a legend that has also persisted. Benne seeds, here, are used to make a sweet wafer.

1/2 cup sesame seeds
3/4 cup butter
1 1/2 cups brown sugar
2 eggs
1 teaspoon vanilla extract
1 1/4 cups all purpose flour
1/4 teaspoon baking powder

Combine all ingredients. Using a teaspoon, place spoon-size dollops of the mixture onto a non-stick baking sheet and bake at 350 degrees for 10 minutes.

164

Boathouse Chocolate Mousse
Serves 6

Lowcountry residents have a remarkable sweet tooth as evidenced by their careful attention to desserts in family receipt and cookbooks over the centuries. This simple dessert finishes nicely with a white chocolate ganache.

FOR THE CRUST:
2 cups Oreo cookie crumbs
3 ounces melted butter

Mix together the butter and crumbs until butter is well absorbed. Spread the mixture evenly into the bottom of a greased 10-inch spring form pan and press until well packed. Place in 350-degree oven for 5 minutes and then refrigerate to cool. Reserve chilled crust for later use.

FOR THE MOUSSE:
2 whole eggs
6 egg yolks
3 ounces granulated sugar
9 ounces chocolate pistoles
6 ounces unsalted butter
1 1/4 ounces cocoa powder
1 1/3 cups heavy cream
1 1/2 ounces Kahlua

In a small mixing bowl, whip heavy cream to soft peaks and set aside for later use. In a medium-sized mixing bowl, whip together sugar and eggs until they double in volume. Melt the chocolate and butter together in a double boiler. Whisk melted chocolate/butter mixture into the eggs. Add cocoa powder and mix well. Gently fold in the whipped cream and then, lastly, the Kahlua. Pour mixture into the pre-formed crust and refrigerate overnight.

FOR THE WHITE CHOCOLATE GANACHE:
15 ounces white chocolate pistoles
5 ounces heavy cream

In a double boiler, melt the white chocolate pistoles. Vigorously whisk the heavy cream into melted white chocolate. Once thoroughly combined, remove from heat and reserve at room temperature.

TO FINISH THE CAKE:
Unlatch the spring form pan and place mousse cake on flat cookie sheet with edges. Using a ladle or spoon, coat cake with the ganache. Return cake to the refrigerator for 1 hour. Slice into 10 even slices with a warm knife to serve.

CHEF'S TIP:
Fill a large pitcher with hot tap water and dip the knife in the water after each cut, using a kitchen towel to dry excess water from the knife.

Buttermilk Ginger Cake, Candied Kumquats, Spiced Crème Fraiche & Caramel Sauce

Serves 6-8

Ginger cakes have long been popular in the Lowcountry, found in many recipe books written in the 18th and 19th centuries. Emily Wharton Sinkler's receipt book from the 1840s includes a thin ginger cake. Early 20th century *Old Receipts from Old St. John's* includes a ginger cake recipe from Wappaoolah Plantation. Though dressed and appointed more luxuriously than earlier recipes, this buttermilk ginger cake is offered in honor of the delicious efforts that have preceded us.

FOR THE CAKE:

1/4 cup butter
1/2 cup sugar
1 egg, well-beaten
1/2 cup molasses
1 2/3 cups flour
1/2 teaspoon baking soda
1/2 teaspoon nutmeg
1 teaspoon baking powder
1 tablespoon ginger
1/2 teaspoon salt
1/2 cup buttermilk
2 tablespoons sugar
1 teaspoon cinnamon

Cream butter and sugar thoroughly, then add the egg and molasses. Add the next six ingredients, alternately with the buttermilk, and beat until smooth. Pour into buttered 9-inch pan, filling the pan only half way. (The mixture will rise.) Sprinkle the top with sugar and cinnamon and bake at 350 degrees for about 45 minutes. Once the center is mostly firm, remove cake from oven and cool to room temperature for slicing. Cut into 6 to 8 equal-sized pieces.

FOR THE KUMQUATS:

8 kumquats, 1/4 inch sliced
2 cups water
2 cups granulated sugar
1 whole vanilla bean

Combine water and sugar, then cook over medium heat until mixture is clear to make simple syrup. Scrape insides of vanilla bean into simple syrup. Place kumquats in simple syrup and increase heat until the kumquat/simple syrup mixture starts to boil. Immediately reduce heat to low and cook for 10 minutes, or until the kumquats are translucent. Remove from heat and allow kumquats to come to room temperature in the syrup. Reserve at room temperature for later use.

FOR THE SPICED CRÈME FRAICHE:

1 cup crème fraiche
2 tablespoons sugar
1/2 teaspoon ground cardamom
1/2 teaspoon ground cinnamon
1/2 teaspoon vanilla paste or extract

Put all ingredients in a bowl and whisk until thick and the mixture holds stiff peaks. (The mixture will get softer before it thickens.) Reserve for later use.

FOR THE CARAMEL SAUCE:

1 1/2 cups heavy cream
3/4 cup butter
1/2 cup dark brown sugar

Combine all ingredients in a heavy-bottomed sauce pan and bring to a boil over medium-high heat. Reduce heat to medium and cook for 8 to10 more minutes or until the mixture is thick. Reserve the caramel sauce at room temperature for later use.

TO FINISH THE DESSERT:

Spoon 2 to 3 ounces of the caramel sauce into the center of a serving plate. Place one piece of cake on top of the caramel sauce. Top the cake with the spiced crème fraiche and garnish with a few of the candied kumquats.

166

Chocolate-Praline Charlotte
With Butterscotch Sauce
Serves 6-8

Charlotte Russe is thought to have been invented by the French chef Marie Antoine Careme (1784-1833), naming it in honor of Alexander I of Russia. Food writer John Martin Taylor suggests this favored dessert may have found its way to Charleston by Lowcountry native Henry Middleton, when he served as United States minister to Russia. However it arrived, by 1847, Sara Rutledge had two Charlotte recipes in her cookbook. Instead of the traditional Bavarian cream, we've put a decidedly Southern touch to this dessert.

FOR THE CHARLOTTE:
6 to 8 ladyfingers, store bought are acceptable
1/4 cup milk
2 teaspoons powdered, unflavored gelatin
1/2 cup plus 2 tablespoons Frangelico liqueur
1 cup chopped bittersweet chocolate
2 1/4 cups heavy cream
1 teaspoon vanilla extract
1/2 cup toasted, chopped pecans

Lightly grease a soufflé or baking dish. Arrange the ladyfingers end to end around the edge, ensuring the darker side faces out. With the 2 tablespoons of the Frangelico, brush each ladyfinger gently. Pour the milk into a sauce pan. Sprinkle gelatin over the milk and let stand for 5 minutes. Add the remaining Frangelico and put on medium-low heat, then stir to dissolve the gelatin. Allow to cool. In a small bowl, melt the chocolate over a double boiler or in the microwave on low heat. In a hand-held mixer, stand mixer or by hand, whip the heavy cream to medium peaks. Add about 1/4 of the whipped cream to the melted chocolate using a whisk to incorporate. Add 1/4 more of the whipped cream using the same technique. Repeat this process until all the chocolate is mixed with the whipped cream. Slowly fold the cooled gelatin mixture

into the whipped cream and chocolate mixture. Repeat the process with the vanilla extract, then carefully fold in the chopped pecans. Fill the mold with the batter and refrigerate for at least 2 hours. Remove from mold carefully by inverting it on a plate. Turn over for presentation and serve with butterscotch sauce.

FOR THE BUTTERSCOTCH SAUCE:
3/4 cup sugar
4 tablespoons water
3/4 cup heavy cream
2 tablespoons butter
1/2 teaspoon vanilla extract

Combine the sugar and water and bring to a simmer. Simmer the mixture for 8 to 10 minutes. The mixture should have an amber color to it. Remove from heat and, while whisking constantly, add the cream a little at a time. Finally, whisk in the butter and vanilla extract. Allow to cool slightly before serving.

167

Research tells us that 14 out of any 10 individuals likes chocolate.

- Sandra Boynton

HOW TO TURN YOUR CHARCOAL GRILL INTO A TOP-NOTCH SMOKER

At the Boathouse, we use a commercial electric-fired smoker for all our in-house smoking – it is consistent and accurate. While store-bought versions for home are available, we recommend using a charcoal grill with quality hardwood charcoal instead. The aroma of the coals and the flavor it infuses can't be beat. Here is a simple way to turn your charcoal grill into a top-notch smoker:

1. Build a fire just like you would for steaks or a pork loin.

2. Once the coals have stopped burning and the embers are bright red, close all dampers except for the one furthest from the fire. Leave it open one half inch. Place the lid back on the grill.

3. Using an appropriate thermometer, and following the guidelines below, monitor the grill to reach the appropriate smoking temperature. Open or close the dampers as necessary to influence the coals until the desired temperature is reached.

4. Open the lid, apply the pre-soaked wood chips to the embers and close the lid.

5. Once the chips have had about 5 minutes on the coals, open the lid, place whatever you are smoking on the rack and close the lid.

6. Check every 15 to 20 minutes to ensure the fire is consistent and the smoking is progressing.

7. Once the smoking is complete, remove from the grill and let rest for 15 to 30 minutes.

For gas grills: Follow the directions above. The only modification would be to apply the chips directly to the lava rocks once the grill has reached the optimum temperature. There is no need to preheat and then lower the temperature.

TEMPERATURE RANGES FOR SMOKING:

ITEM	TEMPERATURE	LENGTH OF TIME
Poultry:	185-220 degrees	15-18 minutes/pound
Fish (cured):	140-155 degrees	5-8 minutes/pound
Fish (uncured):	160-175 degrees	7-10 minutes/pound
Pork:	160-185 degrees	20-30 minutes/pound
Beef:	140-170 degrees	7-10 minutes/pound

Notes: An internal temperature of 180 degrees is recommended for poultry, and 160 to 165 degrees for pork. Smoke beef using these guidelines to your desired level of doneness.

Keep in mind that many things can factor in to the performance of your smoker – whether you're using gas or charcoal, the type of coals and outside temperature. Enjoy!

OUR RESTAURANTS

The original Boathouse restaurant – Boathouse at Breach Inlet, located on the Isle of Palms – opened in October of 1997. Breach Inlet is significant in Lowcountry history because it was the launch site for the Hunley, the celebrated Confederate submarine that sank the USS Housatonic in 1864.

As I developed the concept for the restaurant, I vowed to stay loyal to the basic Southern food upon which I was raised – fresh local seafood prepared simply. Though it may seem strange today, few restaurants in Charleston at the time offered fresh seafood. The majority of the so-called seafood restaurants offered mostly frozen seafood, fried. Dishes that are common today, like wreck bass, wild salmon and Arctic char, were virtually unknown in local restaurants in 1997.

The original structure on the property was a ramshackle bait shop on a beautiful point overlooking the water. We had a great team – architect Reggie Gibson, general manager Sam Richardson, executive chef Jeff Lanzaro, master craftsman Bucky Greelish, master boatbuilder Lawrence Waring, jack-of-all-trades Will Traver, Cousins Construction Company and many others. The restaurant interior and exterior were designed to reflect an understated, beach structure, with a blend of indigenous nautical features.

We hit on a new idea for how to offer the menu – diners could choose daily from five to six different types of fresh fish and from an equal number of preparation styles, such as tarragon butter, blackened or pesto. Additionally, we offered the choice of two of five sides, such as collards or a wonderful Boathouse invention – blue cheese coleslaw. The concept was good, and the blue cheese slaw divine – such that at least half a dozen Lowcountry restaurants have followed suit.

The opening of the first Boathouse inspired another. In February 1999, we acquired a 150-year-old warehouse in downtown Charleston, now home to the Boathouse on East Bay. In keeping with the more sophisticated architecture of

the historic peninsula of Charleston, we sought to create an upscale version of her island sister. Brazilian cherry, aged mahogany, teak and heart pine were selected for the restaurant's interior, mirroring some of the finest aspects of the wooden boats that once graced Charleston Harbor. We dressed the walls with captivating black and white photographs of local nautical history. Two very large paintings were commissioned, depicting the 1929 Carolina Yacht Club Regatta with Castle Pinckney in the background. The spacious setting allowed room for a handsome marble serpentine raw bar where delicious fresh seafood and sushi are served daily.

The mountains of the Carolinas, most especially the Hendersonville/Asheville area, have always felt like home to me. In 2001, the tug of those mountains brought me to Lake Julian, located on the far southern side, or as I tell people, the Charleston side of Asheville. The breathtaking site was a two-and-a-half-acre lakefront tract with stunning views. My brother Ted and I purchased the property and designed a restaurant to echo many of the late 19th- and early 20th-century mountain architectural features, with a lake or camp flare. Massive stone entrance columns were built using a dry-stack method and complemented by hand-made copper gas lanterns. The stone theme was repeated on the walkways and the entire foundation.

One of our interior trademarks has been the variety of wooden antique boats suspended from the ceilings of our restaurants. In the summer of 2001, my wife Lori and young daughter Croft helped me cover some 1,500 miles in Maine in search of antique boats and canoes. We traversed numerous uncharted back roads and ultimately ferreted out four magnificent crafts, the newest of which was built in 1939. These maritime works of art today grace the Boathouse at Lake Julian, along with an elegant 1920s wooden rowing shell suspended over the bar.

It has always been our goal to ensure that each restaurant finds its particular identity. In that vein, we have painstakingly sought out exceptional properties, each with its own individual exterior and interior. Even the uniforms are unique to each location. Beyond the core name Boathouse, we strive to ensure that the dining experience at any one of the three Boathouses is as enjoyable as the others, but none a carbon copy of any other. All three Boathouse restaurants are operated under the umbrella of Crew Carolina,* our management company, or "Crew" as we often call it.

In March 2004, we embarked on another adventure with the acquisition of Carolina's Restaurant, located in a beautiful historic building at 10 Exchange Street in downtown Charleston. Carolina's has been a landmark in Charleston's culinary history since it opened in 1987. The pre-Revolutionary pink stucco building is as rich in local lore as it is in culinary tradition.

Prior to housing Carolina's, the same building was home to Perdita's Restaurant from 1953 to 1987. The only fine dining restaurant in the old city ever located south of Broad Street, Perdita's garnered a number of prestigious international

171

awards including the highly coveted Counsel of Paris Medal of Honor and a National Award of Distinction from *Holiday Magazine.*

Perdita's was unquestionably the premiere restaurant in Charleston from the time it opened in 1953. In a 1967 *New York Times* article, famed food critic Craig Claiborne wrote, "Perhaps the most talked-about and the best of Charleston's restaurants is Perdita's on Exchange Street, a comfortable place with candlelight, exposed brick walls and a feeling of age ... ."

Even the name "Perdita's" is steeped in Charleston lore. The restaurant was named for the beautiful English actress Mrs. Paul Robinson, who became famous for her portrayal of Perdita in Shakespeare's The Winter's Tale. Charleston legend has it that two men – a Charleston gentleman and a New England poet – fought a mortal duel over the 18th-century temptress.

Carolina's replaced Perdita's in 1987, opening with Chef Rose Durden, highly regarded for her classic Southern and

172

traditional Charleston dishes. Many of her dishes carried an Asian flair, reflecting her Vietnamese background. In October 2005, Chef Durden retired and was replaced by Chef Tin Dizdarevic, formerly of Craftbar in New York City. That same year, Crew Carolina launched another division, an off-premise catering company, which we named Carolina Catering. Led by the skilled and talented partner/Executive Chef Phil Corr, Carolina Catering opened to rave reviews, offering a variety of food and accompaniments for parties, from dinner for eight to 500.

Another important endeavor by Crew Carolina is Blue Water Management, Inc., formed to launch a retail line of food products from the Boathouse and Carolina's. These products currently include Blue Cheese Pita Chips, Worcestershire Sauce, Hoisin Ginger Sauce, Steak Sauce, Green Tabasco Cream Sauce and others. The food line is available at select retail locations and online (pgs. 177-178).

The Boathouse Restaurant products speak to our founding concept of foods prepared simply. You'll find all of these items in use at our restaurants; some of them have been on the dinner menu at Breach Inlet since the day we opened. Soon, Carolina's Restaurant will debut its own line of specialty products. Boathouse Collard Greens, Boathouse Benne Seed Wafers, and other traditional food favorites are all products in the works.

In 2007, Crew Carolina launched another venture, providing food service at historic Boone Hall Plantation, a lavish Southern plantation located on the shores of the Cooper River. Boone Hall is one of America's oldest working, living plantations, producing crops for more than 320 years. Once known for cotton and pecans, the plantation now produces peaches, strawberries, tomatoes and pumpkins. We have added

our culinary style to the Boone Hall experience for all who visit. Crew organizes the many catered events held at Boone Hall and has re-opened Serena's Kitchen, the plantation's famed restaurant. Named for Serena Jefferson Spann, an African-American woman, the kitchen features the foods Serena prepared at the plantation for 55 years. The youngest of 18 children, Serena was born in Virginia and was brought to Boone Hall in 1864, the year of her birth. She remained a fixture on the plantation until her death in 1936. Serena's talent as a cook was widely known and much appreciated. She was noted for her biscuits, cinnamon rolls, boiled ham biscuits, shrimp-fried-rice topped with eggs and bacon, layer lemon cakes, potato pone and "pig in the bag."

Serena's Kitchen will re-open as a family-style restaurant serving great lowcountry dishes "plantation-style." True to the premise of Crew Carolina's "simply fresh" philosophy, the restaurant will utilize fresh ingredients from Boone Hall farm and Kensington Plantation. The restaurant will use the freshest seasonal foods and serve them in a manner true to Serena's legacy as a great Lowcountry cook.

With the Boone Hall relationship in place, Crew Carolina established a relationship with a second plantation, this time on the Ashley River. Magnolia Plantation was founded in 1676 by the Drayton family and opened to tourists in 1872, the first site in the Lowcountry to do so. Known for its magnificent gardens and beautiful grounds, the Hastie family, owners of the plantation, invited Crew Carolina to coordinate weddings and catered events. These special events are held on the veranda of the main house, the carriage house and the remodeled conservatory.

A fourth Boathouse restaurant is also in the works. This property, located in downtown Greenville, South Carolina, will be named The Boathouse on the Falls. Establishing a Boathouse restaurant in Greenville is true to the storyline of this cookbook – the migration of the coastal people to the upcountry. Greenville residents have long enjoyed our Boathouse restaurants in Charleston and Asheville. We're now pleased to join the culinary community in the South Carolina upstate with our latest venture.

Much like the recipes presented in this book, exceptional things occur when the right combination of ingredients is brought together. The same is certainly true for Crew Carolina and our culinary outlets. We are fortunate to be joined by a number of passionate and talented people who comprise our team. Passion for food and service to our customers will always be a prerequisite to joining Crew. Our ranks have grown to more than 200, who daily work to bring the best of our native foods from our table to your palate. We hope you enjoy the experience!

175

BOATHOUSE PRODUCTS

Boathouse Worcestershire Sauce
12 ounces

Boathouse Worcestershire combines citrus, hot peppers and sweet onions for a sauce unlike any other Worcestershire. Perfect for meat and fish fresh off the grill or out of the oven or use as a marinade for your favorite cut of meat.

Boathouse Steak Sauce
12 ounces

A bold and hearty blend perfect for the finest cuts of beef, chicken or pork straight off your grill. Also great on burgers and chicken sandwiches.

Boathouse Hoisin-Ginger Sauce
12 ounces

Sweet and sour blend of ginger, hoisin sauce, teriyaki and pineapple juice. Works beautifully in garden salads and stir fry. Also try with grilled or blackened fish or chicken.

Boathouse Green Tabasco Cream Sauce
16 ounces

A zesty blend of cream, Tabasco Brand Green Tabasco sauce, lemon juice and shallots. Gives a delightful edge to crab cakes, seared fresh fish, and as a finish for shrimp and grits.

177

Boathouse Blue Cheese Chips

6 ounces

Crispy flat bread chips with crumbled blue cheese baked into every chip. Delicious with seafood dips and spreads or straight out of the bag.

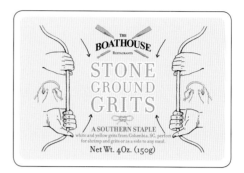

Boathouse Grits:

16 ounces

A true Southern staple. The Boathouse blend of stone ground white and yellow grits from Columbia, South Carolina, make for a truly tasty shimp and grits. Or have it as a side to your favorite meal.

178

Boathouse "Best Ever" Collard Greens:

16 fluid ounces

These collards aren't just for New Year's anymore! The sweetness of brown sugar and the tartness and spice of red wine vinegar and Tabasco sauce make these the "best ever" collards.

Boathouse Blackening Seasoning:

5 ounces

A Boathouse classic. Add some heat to your shrimp and grits or "blacken" a fresh filet of fish.

To order Boathouse products, go to www.boathouserestaurants.com or call 888-576-BOAT (2628).

PHOTOGRAPHY & IMAGE CREDITS

The authors are grateful to the following friends and institutions for granting the privilege to publish select images from their collections:

Douglas W. Bostick and Daniel J. Crooks from their collection published in *On the Eve of the Charleston Renaissance: The George W. Johnson Photographs:*
Pg. 12 – "Adger's Wharf, circa 1910"
Pg. 22 – "Hunting Party on Morris Island"
Pg. 25 – "Rainbow Row, circa 1914"
Pg. 28 – "Vegetable Children"
Pg. 31 – "Sunday Afternoon at Sullivan's Island"

South Carolina Historical Society:
Pg. 13 – Medway Plantation
Pg. 14 – 29 East Battery
Pg. 15 – View from the porch of 29 East Battery.

Library of Congress:
Pg. 21– Grove Park Inn fireplace
Pg. 26 – Mountain family

Author's Collection:
Pg. 27– Fishing in McClellanville

United States Senate Collection:
Pg. 101 – "General Marion Inviting a British Officer to Share His Meal"

Dr. Merle Sheppard, Professor of Entomology, Clemson University
Pg. 105 – Carolina Gold Rice

All other photographs are by Stewart Young.

Reproduction of the following original paintings is granted by artist West Fraser and Fraser Fox Fine Art, 12 Queen Street, Charleston, SC:
Pg. 42 – "It's a Beautiful Garden"
Pg. 76 – "Support American Fishermen"
Pg. 106 – "Taylor with a Double"
Pg. 146 – "Red Light"

179

BIBLIOGRAPHY

"Bad Roads, Loose Morals, Sadism, and Racetrack Discipline, 1830." *South Carolina: The Grand Tour,* 1780-1865. Ed. Thomas D. Clark. Columbia, SC: University of South Carolina Press, 1970.

Bailey, David Coleman. *Fashionable Asheville.* Charleston, SC: BookSurge, 2004.

Bailey, Louise Howe. Personal Interview. November 2005.

Bailey, Louise Howe. *Remembering Henderson County: A Legacy of Lore.* Charleston: History Press, 2005.

Bailey, Louise Howe. *St. John's in the Wilderness, 1836 - .* Asheville, NC: Biltmore Press, 1995.

Bolitho, Hector. *The Glorious Oyster.* New York: Alfred A. Knopf, 1929.

Bostick, Douglas W. and Daniel J. Crooks Jr. *On the Eve of the Charleston Renaissance: The George W. Johnson Photographs.* Charleston, SC: Joggling Board Press, 2005.

Bostick, Douglas. *Secession to Siege 1860/1865: The Charleston Engravings.* Charleston, SC: Joggling Board Press, 2004.

Boynton, Sandra. *Chocolate: The Consuming Passion.* New York: Workman Publishing Co., 1982.

Brewster, Lawrence Fay. *Summer Migrations and Resorts of South Carolina Low-Country Planters.* Durham, NC: Duke University Press, 1947.

Bryan, Bill. *Folly Beach: Glimpses of a Vanished Strand.* Charleston, SC: History Press, 2005.

Burger, Ann. *South Carolina: Always in Season.* Kuttawa, KY: McClanahan Publishing House, 2002.

Burrell, Victor G. Jr. *South Carolina Oyster Industry: A History.* Charleston, SC: Author, 2003.

Carlton, Mrs. Helen T. *The Practical and Family Cookbook for Every Household.* Louisville, KY: Press of Courier-Journal, 1942.

Charleston Receipts. Charleston, SC: The Junior League of Charleston, 1950.

Collins, Willis E. *Sentenia.* Unpublished manuscript, 1947.

Dabney, Joseph Earl. *Mountain Spirits.* Ashville, NC: Bright Mountain Books, 1974.

Dabney, Joseph E. *Smokehouse Ham, Spoonbread & Scuppernong Wine: The Folklore and Art of Southern Appalachian Cooking.* Nashville, TN: Cumberland House, 1998.

DuBose, J. E. *Receipt Book,* DuBose Family Papers, 1790 – 1904. Charleston, SC: South Carolina Historical Society, unpublished.

Egerton, John. *Side Orders: Small Helpings of Southern Cookery and Culture.* Atlanta, GA: Peachtree Publishers, 1990.

Egerton, John. *Southern Food: At Home, on the Road, in History.* Chapel Hill, NC: University of North Carolina Press, 1993.

Egerton, John. *The Endurance of Southern Food.* Oxford American Spring 2005: 18 – 20.

Ehler, James T. 2006 <http://foodreference.com>.

Fishburne, Anne Sinkler, ed. *Old Receipts from Old St. Johns.* Unpublished manuscript.

181

Fraser, Walter J. *Charleston! Charleston!: The History of a Southern City*. Columbia, SC: University of South Carolina Press, 1989.

Gilbert, John E. and Jeffreys, Grady. *Crossties over Saluda*. Raleigh, NC: Crossties Press, 1971.

Hess, Karen. *The Carolina Rice Kitchen: The African Connection*. Columbia, SC: University of South Carolina Press, 1992.

Horry, Brig. Gen. P. and M. L. Weems. *The Life of General Francis Marion*. Philadelphia: J. B. Lippincott & Co., 1879.

Hutchisson, James M., and Harlan Greene, eds. *Renaissance in Charleston: Art and Life in the Carolina Lowcountry, 1900-1940*. Athens, GA: University of Georgia Press, 2003.

Irving, John Beaufain. *A Day on the Cooper River*. Columbia: R. L. Bryan Co., 1969.

Irving, Dr. John Beaufain. *The South Carolina Jockey Club*. Charleston, SC: Russel & Jones, 1857.

LeClercq, Anne Sinkler Whaley. *An Antebellum Household: Including the South Carolina Low Country Receipts and Remedies of Emily Wharton Sinkler*. Columbia, SC: University of South Carolina Press, 1996.

Leiding, Harriette Kershaw. *Charleston Historic and Romantic*. Philadelphia: J. B. Lippincott Co., 1931.

Leland, John A. *A Voice from South Carolina*. Charleston, SC: Walker, Evans & Cogswell, 1879.

Lesesne, Thomas Petigru. *Landmarks of Charleston Including Description of an Incomparable Stroll*. Richmond, VA: Garrett & Massie, 1939.

McCullers, Carson. *The Member of the Wedding*. New York: Houghton Mifflin, 1946.

McDaniel, Rick. Personal Interview. November 2005.

McDaniel, Rick. "Replanting the rice known as Carolina Gold." *Asheville Citizen-Times* 19 October 2005, C1+.

Memminger, Edward Read. *An Historical Sketch of Flat Rock*. Privately published by Mrs. Walter M. Norment, 1954.

Milne, A. A. *The House at Pooh Corner*. New York: E. P. Dutton, 1988.

Mitter, Siddhartha. "Free Okra." *Oxford American* (Spring 2005): 59 - 60.

Native American Foods and Cookery. Raleigh, NC: NC State Museum of Natural Science, 1986.

Neal, William F. *Bill Neal's Southern Cooking*. Chapel Hill, NC: University of North Carolina Press, 1985.

Neufeld, Rob. Personal Interview. November 2005.

Osbourne, Anne and Charlene Pace. *Saluda, NC: One Hundred Years, 1881 – 1991*. Saluda, NC: Holly Hill Publishers, 1981.

Parris, John. *Mountain Cooking*. Asheville, NC: Citizen-Times Publishing Co., 1978.

Patton, Sadie Smathers. *A Condensed History of Flat Rock*. Flat Rock, NC: Historic Flat Rock, Inc., n.d.

Platt, Loula Roberts. *Queen of Appalachia Cookbook*. Batavia, NY: Press of Batavia Times, n.d.

Ravenel, Rose P. *Charleston Recollections and Receipts*. Elizabeth Ravenel Harrigan, ed. Sewanee, TN: Lollyett & Rogers, 1983.

Recipe Book of Eliza Lucas Pinckney, 1756. Charleston, SC: Charleston Lithographing Company, 1936.

Reuther, Galen. *Flat Rock: The Little Charleston of the Mountains*. Charleston, SC: Arcadia Publishing, 2004.

Rhett, Blanche S. *Two Hundred Years of Charleston Cooking*. Columbia, SC: University of South Carolina Press, 1976.

Robertson, William H. P. *The History of Thoroughbred Racing in America*. New York: Bonanza Books, 1964.

Rogers, Amy. *Hungry for Home*. Charlotte, NC: Novello Festival Press, 2003.

Rogers, George C. Jr. *Charleston in the Age of the Pinckneys.* Columbia, SC: University of South Carolina Press, 1980.

Rosen, Robert N. *A Short History of Charleston.* San Francisco: Lexikos, 1982.

Rutledge, Sarah. *The Carolina Housewife.* Charleston, SC: W. R. Babcock & Co., 1847.

Shelton, Ferne, ed. *Southern Appalachian Mountain Cookbook.* High Point, NC: Hutcraft, 1964.

Shuptrine, Hubert and James Dickey. *Jericho.* Birmingham, AL: Oxmoor House, 1974.

Simms, W. Gilmore. *The Life of Francis Marion.* New York: Derby & Jackson, 1858.

Sohn, Mark F. *Mountain Cooking.* New York: St. Martin's Press, 1996.

Stoney Family Receipt Book. Stoney Family Papers. Charleston, SC: South Carolina Historical Society, unpublished.

Stoney Family Notebook, 1888 – 1916. Stoney Family Papers. Charleston, SC: South Carolina Historical Society, unpublished.

Stoney, Mrs. Samuel G., ed. *Carolina Rice Cookbook.* Charleston, SC: Carolina Rice Kitchen Association, 1901.

Stradley, Linda. *What's Cooking America.* 2004 <http://whatscookingamerica.net>.

Taylor, John Martin. *Hoppin' John's Lowcountry Cooking.* New York: Bantam Books, 1992.

Taylor, Teresa. "In a League of its Own." *The Post and Courier* 2 November 2005, D1+.

Twain, Mark. *The Autobiography of Mark Twain.* New York: Harper, 1959.

The Spirit of the Times 11 February 1860.

Verner, Elizabeth O'Neill. *Mellowed by Time: A Charleston Notebook.* Charleston, SC: Tradd Street Press, 1978.

Walter, Eugene. "An Ode to Figs." *Oxford American* (Spring 2005): 33.

Whaley, Emily. *Mrs. Whaley's Charleston Kitchen: Advice, Opinions, and 100 Recipes from a Southern Legend.* New York: Simon & Schuster, 1998.

Wilson, Lawrence. "Swamp Gig." *Oxford American* (Spring 2005): 12.

Wilson, Robert. *Half-Forgotten By-Ways of the Old South.* Columbia, SC: The State Co., 1928.

Wolfe, Thomas. *Look Homeward, Angel.* New York: Scribner, 1997.

183

RECIPE INDEX

185

SUBJECT INDEX

187

188

189

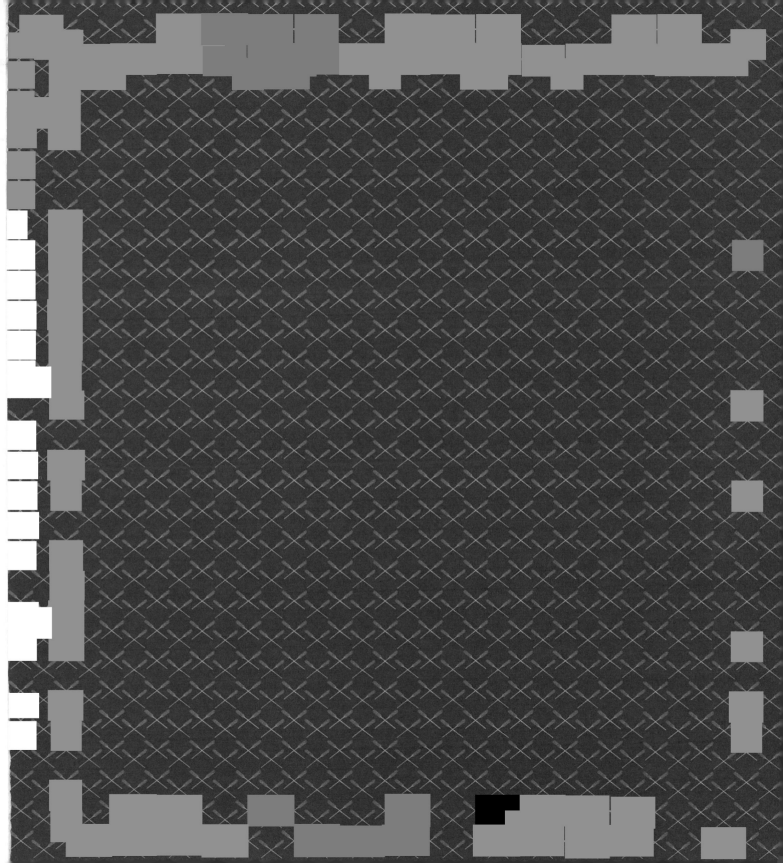